"Justine Doiron's debut book *Justine Cooks* is innovative and inspiring. Whether you're a new or seasoned cook, this book gets you excited to be in the kitchen and Justine is alongside rooting you on."

—COLU HENRY, author of *Back Pocket Pasta* and *Colu Cooks: Easy Fancy Food*

"*Justine Cooks* is like your culinary buddy, encouraging you to try those daring flavor combos or master techniques you thought were out of reach. It's an indispensable guide for both seasoned chefs and home cooking enthusiasts alike. Get ready to be inspired."

—CARLA HALL, chef personality and author of *Carla Hall's Soul Food*

"Whether you've been following and loving on Justine Snacks for years (hi, that's me!) or are just discovering her here, you are in for a gorgeous and delicious cornucopia of genius cooking tips, flavor combos, recipes, and more. For me, it was the 'obsessive chocolate chip cookie behavior' spread that confirmed Justine and I are indeed ~~soul~~ snack sisters."

—JESSIE SHEEHAN, author of *Salty, Cheesy, Herby, Crispy Snackable Bakes*

"Apologies to my mother, who tried very hard, but no one can get me to eat my vegetables like Justine. In *Justine Cooks*, her plant-forward recipes are intensely crunchy, creamy, crispy, and crave-worthy. Meet me at the farmers' market, ladies, it's *go* time!"

—DAN PELOSI, author of *Let's Eat*

"This cookbook quite literally set my brain whirring and my mouth watering and basically left me unfit for anything other than cooking my way through it immediately. I do not exaggerate. Dates are torn. Harissa eggplant is drippy. Poached eggs are kimchi crusted. The green beans are frizzled, the shallots are sticky, and the tomato beans are hotties (and they know it)."

—DAPHNE OZ, bestselling cookbook author and Emmy award-winning television host

"Not only is this book beautiful, but Justine's approach to cooking makes me crave vegetables in ways I never knew I could. These recipes are flavor bombs with thoughtful steps to make ordinary ingredients shine in a way that meat would only play second fiddle to. I imagine finding this book dog-eared and stained in my kitchen for years to come."

—NINI NGUYEN, chef and author of *Đặc Biệt: An Extra-Special Vietnamese Cookbook*

JUSTINE COOKS

JUSTINE COOKS

Recipes (Mostly Plants) for
Finding Your Way in the Kitchen

Justine Doiron

Photographs by Jim Henkens

CLARKSON POTTER/PUBLISHERS

NEW YORK

Copyright © 2024 by Justine Doiron
Photographs copyright © 2024 by Jim Henkens

Published in the United States by Clarkson Potter/Publishers, an
imprint of the Crown Publishing Group, a division of Penguin
Random House LLC, New York.
ClarksonPotter.com

CLARKSON POTTER is a trademark and POTTER with colophon
is a registered trademark of Penguin Random House LLC.

Library of Congress Cataloging-in-Publication Data
Names: Doiron, Justine, author. | Henkens, Jim, photographer.
Title: Justine Cooks : recipes, essays, and stories, all about : starting
from scratch / Justine Doiron ; photographs by Jim Henkens.
Description: New York : Clarkson Potter/Publishers, [2024] |
Includes index. | Identifiers: LCCN 2023048013 (print) | LCCN
2023048014 (ebook) | ISBN 9780593582305 (hardcover) | ISBN
9780593582312 (ebook) Subjects: LCSH: Cooking. | LCGFT:
Cookbooks. Classification: LCC TX714 .D5455 2024 (print) | LCC
TX714 (ebook) | DDC 641.5—dc23/eng/20240314
LC record available at https://lccn.loc.gov/2023048013
LC ebook record available at https://lccn.loc.gov/2023048014

ISBN 978-0-5935-8230-5
Ebook ISBN 978-0-5935-8231-2

Printed in China

Editor: Susan Roxborough
Editorial assistant: Elaine Hennig
Production editor: Ashley Pierce
Production manager: Jessica Heim
Compositors: Merri Ann Morrell and Hannah Hunt
Food stylist: Frances Boswell
Food stylist assistants: Young Gun Lee and Sofia Toddeo
Prop stylist: Brooke Deonarine
Copyeditor: Dolores York
Proofreader: Sasha Tropp
Indexer: Ken DellaPenta
Publicist: Natalie Yera-Campbell
Marketer: Brianne Sperber

10 9 8 7 6 5 4 3 2 1

First Edition

TO ERIC, IT WAS ALWAYS YOURS

CONTENTS

INTRODUCTION

IT WAS AN ITALIAN-STYLE SALSA VERDE THAT CHANGED ME.

I realize that it's a kind of choice to start my book by talking about a condiment, but in this case, it's *fitting*. That's because, as I was trying to pinpoint the exact moment when I fell in love with food, I kept going back to a single recipe—parsley, capers, shallot, garlic, lemon, and olive oil. Taste, season, adjust, and repeat.

For context, I'm a person who didn't grow up in a food family. We enjoyed food, but it wasn't a part of us. I never had a fresh herb until my twenties, because before then? Well, it sure seemed like a frivolous way to run up a grocery bill. So, when I started to learn more about food—its history, the cultures that surround it, and the many different methods of preparing it—it opened up a whole new (and delicious) world.

And the salsa verde? Well, that zesty little Italian sauce came into my life after combing through one too many cookbooks (which okay, *yes*, there's no such thing) and seeing that my favorite authors all included a salsa verde in their pages. At first, I couldn't understand the hype. Salsa/gremolata/relish: They all felt the same to me. But then . . . then, one day I made it.

That one small sauce was the tipping point. Before that, I had been looking at food like a science. I was forcing recipes into rules, strict and precise. But as simple as this recipe was, it was the first flavor combination that showed me how expansive food could be: how an ingredient that felt boring becomes completely transformed when partnered with a few others; how different recipes and methods build beautiful flavors over time; and also, when it's made in my kitchen, how non-formulaic everything becomes. Every ingredient has a story, a pairing, and a way to manipulate and master it. Food became electric, food became comforting, and it was food that took a girl (ahem, me) who didn't have a cooking background and gave her a way to feel at home.

I started cooking online using the jokey name of @Justine_Snacks, sharing what I knew, what I was learning, and why food and eating were so important to me. I talked about how food made me feel as if I were building my own sense of belonging. Along the way, I heard from many people who felt the same way. Cooking bonded us. And while I loved my online name, deep down I knew it was always more than just "snacks."

This book goes past where I started online, past my small apartment, where I tore through cookbooks like novels and textbooks rolled into one. I wrote this book to both connect with other home cooks and to share recipes that, frankly, I'm obsessed with—innovative ideas that you can master and transform. The recipes are technique-driven but accessible. They are repeatable, for easy go-tos, but also transformable, so you can make them your own.

I wrote these recipes for people who are deeply in love with food, but I also wrote them to satiate readers who, just like I once was, are learning and growing in their kitchen and looking for a way to make cooking feel uniquely theirs. These are the recipes I wish I had had when I started cooking: innovative and fun, each equipped with new techniques, methods, and small pockets of things to learn. Cooking is like a muscle, and I want this book to help you flex it. But if it does for only one person what that salsa verde did for me, I'll consider it a success.

HOW I HOPE YOU'LL USE THIS BOOK

COOKBOOKS ARE WRITTEN TO BE WRITTEN ON. Don't get me wrong, each of these recipes has been painstakingly tested to give you the best method, technique, and results, and I'd love for you to cook them exactly as you see them. But I believe after you've made a recipe once, it becomes yours.

I hope these recipes inspire you to trust your palate, adopt new methods, and learn unique flavor combinations so you can copy and paste all of that onto your own ideas. Whether you read this book in bed for inspiration or reference it on your countertop with sticky fingers, I want it to be useful for how you cook now and how you will cook in the future. My greatest hope is that one day you won't even have to reference these recipes, but that parts of them will live in your brain in a way where you can repeat them again and again. A good book should make you go from "I want to make everything in this" to "I wonder how I can tweak this," then continue to return to it as a guide, starting point, and inspiration for your own tried-and-true recipes.

It would make me so happy to have these pages oil-stained and with pencil scribbles on the side—signs of a book well used. Because homemade food isn't just made from scratch. It's food that makes you feel at home.

SMALL KITCHEN, BIG ENERGY

I've loved every kitchen I've lived with. I say "live with" because you live *in* your house (or apartment, or dorm, or wherever), but you really live *with* your kitchen.

My current kitchen is tiny, but I love it. Okay, so I have to rotate and reorganize my pantry every time I buy a new tomato paste. And yes, my utensils live in a place that's either slightly or deeply inconvenient to reach, depending on my mood. But for the most part, I've made this small kitchen support me in all the ways I like to cook.

Whether you have a stove with six burners (I'm jealous) or a hot plate, you can set up your kitchen so you have everything you need to support your cooking. There are certain tools that are a must and certain tools that are a maybe, foods that I recommend you always keep in your cabinets and foods I recommend buying on the day you plan to use them. I also want to share a few key techniques, things I hope you'll keep in mind as you cook through this book, and use again and again in your own cooking, too.

No kitchen is perfect, but I want yours to feel like a practical, comfortable, and intuitive space. Here are the things that improve my space, but take what you want, adapt what you need, and leave the rest behind.

TOOLS THAT YOU CAN (AND ALSO CAN'T) BUY

I don't typically advocate for single-use tools, so all these are multifunctional
and meant to contribute the most for the space they take up. When I splurge
on a tool, I look at it from a cost-per-use perspective, so I'll only recommend the
things I think are absolutely worth the investment. As for the tools you can't buy,
well, you'll find more about those on page 22.

THE DAILIES

(Keep These within
Arm's Reach)

5- TO 6-QUART LARGE POT WITH LID: I mostly use one pot, and this
size seems to cover everyday cooking, plus it makes a great weight for
pressing tofu (see page 207).

12-INCH OVENPROOF STAINLESS STEEL SAUTÉ PAN: This is my
go-to pan. It can be used for frying and whipping up sauces or
small-batch soups, and it lends itself well to one-pan meals (see
page 175 for inspo).

8-INCH SKILLET: This is what I reach for when I want to fry a quick
egg, toast some spices, or fry up garlic chips. If a recipe calls for a small
pan, use this one.

¾-QUART SMALL SAUCEPAN: If I have a quick sauce to make, milk to
scald, butter to brown, or a small batch to reheat, a small saucepan is
easy to use and clean.

NESTED MIXING BOWLS: Nested because my kitchen space is
precious. Make sure they are temperature-safe so you can use them
for double boiling or chilling in an ice bath.

6-INCH CHEF'S KNIFE: This is my all-purpose knife, and I find 5 to
6 inches is the most comfortable for me. Look for a knife that is fully
forged (meaning it's a single rod of steel, tip to end) and three-layer
steel, if your budget allows it.

SPIDER STRAINER OR HANDHELD SIEVE: Good for blanching herbs,
boiling eggs, and lifting pasta out of the water. You'll never have to
navigate a huge pot over a strainer again.

OFFSET SPATULA AND SILICONE SPATULA: Two spatulas that fit all
needs. I like my silicone for folding, scraping, and stirring. The offset is
for lifting, flipping, spreading, and swirling.

RASP-STYLE GRATER: My citrus zester, cheese garnisher, and ginger grater all in one. I use this multiple times a day. It also lies perfectly flat in your utensil drawer, which is always nice.

WHISKS, ONE BIG, ONE SMALL: For whipping, emulsifying, stirring, and even sifting dry ingredients. Just wait until you discover the adorable utility of a tiny whisk: small bowl, small whisk, small cleanup.

BENCH SCRAPER: Great for bread baking but also ideal for scooping up chopped veggies or cleaning your work surface. I treat mine like my left hand; it's always with me.

COOKING TWEEZERS: Thinner than tongs, I like these for things like flipping over eggplant halves, sautéing delicate tofu cubes, or twirling up noodles for plating.

OVEN THERMOMETER: Ovens can be off as much as 25° to 50°F, so keep a thermometer in there to help you monitor and adjust, if needed.

DIGITAL SCALE: Measuring cups are a good starting point (see page 22), but grams are always more accurate, especially when it comes to baking. Using a scale also means fewer dishes: I measure directly into a bowl, reset the scale to zero, and repeat for the next ingredient.

THE SECONDARIES

(Keep These in Tiptoe Reach)

5½-QUART DUTCH OVEN: When I'm making big hearty stews, spaetzle (see page 202), or sourdough (see page 235), this size works best. Get one in a pretty color but know the color will fade as it becomes well used, an earned badge of honor.

12-INCH CAST-IRON SKILLET: For hard searing, high-heat cooking, and oven roasting; it really is a myth that they're hard to take care of.

STAND MIXER: The most expensive thing on this list but such a good investment in a home cook's kitchen. It can knead bread, whip cream in seconds, shred tofu, and smooth out any batter.

SMALL 1-QUART BLENDER: I use this more often than my big blender. It's the perfect size for dressings, sauces, and spreads, plus it's easier to clean. If you own a small blender, it's all you'll need for the recipes in this book. (If you own a big one, that's great, too!)

5-CUP FOOD PROCESSOR: My world changed when I swapped my full-size food processor for a half-size. When your food processor is within reach, sauces become a breeze, and grating large amounts of cheese or vegetables feels less like a chore.

SALAD SPINNER: Dressing can't cling to wet lettuce, and wet herbs will rot really fast in the fridge. Get a salad spinner for everything leafy and green to save on time and food waste. (The basket also works as a great strainer when washing vegetables!)

13 BY 18-INCH HALF-SHEET PANS: Yes, I love my fun-colored ones, but a light-colored, aluminum one will give you much more even bakes.

9½ BY 13-INCH QUARTER-SHEET PANS: A smaller sheet pan for when you have half the amount of ingredients. Voilà!

PRECUT PARCHMENT PAPER: The rule I try to live by: Buy my vegetables whole and my parchment cut. Precut sheets of parchment will save you so many battles with scissors—just trust me.

INSTANT-READ PROBE THERMOMETER: Having a probe thermometer is like having an authority on temperature, whether you're baking, frying, or checking the internal temperature of your fish. I call for certain oil temperatures throughout the book, and I've found hovering the end of my probe thermometer so it's just touching the oil quickly gives me a wildly accurate reading.

VEGETABLE PEELER: I like a Y-peeler for vegetables, of course, but also for thin slices of cheese in salads (see page 114) or for peeling citrus twists for cocktails.

A CARED-FOR CAST-IRON SKILLET

To clean your cast-iron skillet, let it cool slightly, wipe it with paper towels, and then typically, you're done. For any stuck-on bits, use warm water and a gentle brush. For any stubborn bits, add a tablespoon of kosher salt and a splash of vegetable oil to scrub. Dish soap is fine; just know it will strip off some of the seasoning but won't hurt the skillet. After any contact with water, set the skillet over high heat to dry completely. Swirl in some vegetable oil and let it smoke. Remove from the heat and use a paper towel to wipe out the excess oil. Cool completely before storing. Reseason every month or so.

THE FEW AND FAR BETWEENS

(Keep These out of Reach—but Easy to Find)

BAKING DISHES: Both 8 by 8-inch and 9 by 13-inch. Porcelain is old-school and works great. Glass heats slowly, which can make for uneven baking. My favorite is light-colored aluminum-coated steel for perfect browning, whether you're baking savory or sweet.

9-INCH SPRINGFORM PAN: If you're going to get a circular pan, you might as well make it a springform. It releases cakes in a snap (literally), is perfect for quiches or tarts, and I love using mine for Tamarind-Date Bars (page 257).

PROOFING BASKETS: I don't believe in single-use tools, but this is the one exception. If you venture into the world of baking bread (see page 235), you'll need a couple of these.

ROLLING PIN: Great for rolling out crusts but also a killer for smashing potatoes or making crumbs.

THE TOOLS YOU CAN'T BUY

While the physical things are important, there are a few intangible tools that are equally vital. These are four things that have completely changed how I cook.

KEEPING TIME: Cooking is a very flexible and intuitive activity. Visual cues are great indicators, and common sense is king, but sometimes we can underestimate or overestimate by 2 to 3 minutes and completely misread the cues. If you are still stretching your kitchen muscles, keeping time is a great way to guide yourself toward a cook's intuition. It can be as simple as using the timer on your phone or cranking a dedicated kitchen timer. I know a timer has helped me tenfold.

WORKING CLEAN: Working clean means different things for different recipes, but as a rule of thumb, I like to use my bench scraper as I go, to gather any scraps into a compost bowl, and move dishes to the sink to keep my surrounding areas clear. This is the first skill I took away from my college culinary classes, and I swear it makes your food taste better.

KEEP YOUR OVEN CLOSED: Ovens are the best, and ovens are the worst. For a kitchen appliance that hinges on the promise of accuracy, they do a horrible job at staying accurate. Ovens are designed to hit the desired temperature, then shut off. An internal thermometer triggers the next temperature reading, and the oven cranks the heat just enough to climb back up to the desired temperature, and so on and so forth. I won't even get into how that temperature can be way far off (which is why I recommend an oven thermometer; see page 19). So while we can't do much about the temperature, we *can* do our part to keep that hot air circulating. The only time you should open an oven is if the recipe asks you to rotate or at the noted time, to check doneness.

MEASURING WITH YOUR EYE: Notice I didn't include measuring cups in the lists of tools on page 18? My kitchen scale (see page 19) has become my measuring cup for baking, and when it comes to cooking, I cast aside my cups and spoons a long time ago. (I did order some so this book would be accurate!) Learning to eyeball a tablespoon of vinegar and to feel a teaspoon of salt in your palm is a skill that can save you dishes and time, plus build your sensibility as a cook. Next time you measure something dry, pour it into your hand and see how much room it takes. When measuring something liquid, watch as you stream it into the bowl. How long was that pour, and how big of an imprint did it make on the surface? Soon enough, you'll be able to measure by experience instead of by volume.

MY PANTRY AND MY FRIDGE

My pantry is my foundation, and my fridge is my flexibility. My pantry sees the same steady roster, but my fridge is much more in flux, meaning that if an ingredient earns a spot there, it gets used quickly and replaced only when the mood for it strikes again. But if something has made this list, that means it has definitely proven its worth.

PANTRY

SALT: I believe you only need two salts to make food taste delicious. First, a kosher salt. You'll see I use Diamond Crystal in this book. That's because I find easier to work with, since it has a larger grain. If you opt to use a finer grain of kosher salt or sea salt, use about half the amount called for in the recipe. The other salt is a finishing salt with a large flake. Maldon is a popular choice, but emerging brands like FalkSalt produce wonderful versions as well. Use this for finishing, making a crunchy, salty bite.

BLACK PEPPER: Pepper is so common that we forget how transformative it is. Grinding whole peppercorns activates all the oils, spice, and hidden notes in them. I like to use the coarsest setting on my pepper grinder to get big crunchy bits every time.

SPICES AND DRIED HERBS: I replenish these regularly. For example, I can guarantee the dried rosemary that has followed you through three apartment leases is not at its prime. Spices like coriander, cumin, fennel seeds, caraway seeds, and black mustard seeds are spices I buy whole and crush with a mortar and pestle or in a spice grinder, while Aleppo pepper flakes, smoked paprika, and red pepper flakes are spices I purchase ground. These I restock every 3 to 6 months. Store your spices in a cool, dry place.

OILS: I advocate for a big oil and vinegar collection, and once I started shelling out the extra few dollars for the good stuff, my cooking immediately felt the change. I use single-origin extra-virgin olive oil for most of my cooking. My favorite regions to source from are California (ENZO is a great brand), Spain (Graza has a great price point for the quality), and Portugal (ZOE is my favorite single-origin and the bottle

design is gorgeous). Cook with a moderately priced EVOO and save a more expensive, darker oil for dressings, sauces, and a finishing drizzle.

VINEGARS: Brightland, Acid League, and O make great vinegars, and my favorites are champagne, red wine, sherry, apple cider, and balsamic. I'm not saying run out and buy them all, but I will advocate for a good mix. Each one has slightly different levels of sweetness and acidity to add variety to your cooking. Distilled white vinegar is necessary, too, for projects like pickling and cleaning your fridge.

FLOURS, COLLECTIVELY: Like most things, flour performs better when you opt for the higher-quality brands. This is especially true when making things like sourdough starter (see page 231) and bread (see page 235), where the nutrition in the flour is key. King Arthur is my go-to for baking, but Bob's Red Mill also makes great flours. If you are going to start with three kinds of flour, I recommend all-purpose flour, whole-wheat flour, and bread flour. From there, you can expand to dark rye flour, cassava flour, chickpea flour, and cornmeal, all of which can be used in fantastic dishes like the Farofa (page 48), ACV Brussels Sprouts (page 148), and Hominy Biscuits (page 86).

DRIED GRAINS: My pantry is incomplete without an assortment of these grains, such as farro, quinoa, and buckwheat. Rice is also a staple, with short-grain sushi rice being my preferred, and brown rice, wild rice, and Arborio (the rice used for risotto) rounding out my stockpile. Rolled oats are included in my grain selection; these are especially good when I can get them from a small grain mill, but I also dip into the great high-quality brands sold at most grocery stores.

DRIED PASTAS: The brand really does make a difference. I love Sfoglini, but De Cecco is a classic Italian brand that's hella affordable and excellent quality, so I always have a few boxes in my pantry.

DRIED AND CANNED BEANS: I speak about this more in the beans chapter on page 159, but the age of dried beans really does matter! I try to keep the shelf life of my dried beans to a year, since that's the point when their texture, flavor, and cook time begins to be deeply impacted. In the dried-bean realm, heirloom beans are a real treat, so I buy those whenever my budget allows and aim to use them within the month. I always stock a few cans of beans, with my favorites being butter beans, chickpeas, and kidney beans.

SEEDS AND NUTS: I keep a variety of both on hand, including cashews, walnuts, almonds, chia seeds, flaxseeds, and hemp hearts, and I actually keep them in my freezer. Because nuts and seeds have a high oil content, their shelf life is brief, and they can spoil in less than a few months. Freezing keeps them endlessly fresh.

A FEW OTHER THINGS I KEEP IN MY PANTRY

SAVORY AND SPICY THINGS

Sambal oelek

Harissa (mild to hot)

Calabrian chili paste

Ají amarillo paste

Louisiana-style hot sauce
(I'm loyal to Frank's RedHot)

Soy sauce

Tamari

Fish sauce

Worcestershire sauce

Mustard (Dijon and whole-grain)

Olives (such as Kalamata
or Castelvetrano)

Nonpareil capers
(stored in brine)

Sun-dried tomatoes
(stored in oil)

Tomato paste (the tube is
easier than the can)

Preserved lemon paste

Nutritional yeast

Flat-packed anchovy fillets

Canned tuna
(packed in oil, always)

SWEET AND STICKY THINGS

Honey
(or sorghum syrup
or agave nectar)

Fig jam
(rarely any other kind)

Kecap manis
(or any sweet soy sauce)

Mirin

Coconut milk (full-fat)

Tahini

Almond butter
(or any drizzly nut butter)

FRIDGE

EGGS: I source my eggs either from Vital Farms, which I trust implicitly, or from a farmers' market. Happy chickens are always worth the cost.

BUTTER: I like to buy Kerrygold's grass-fed if I can, and only salted butter, which won't oversalt your food. Just think of it as flavor insurance.

DAIRY: It's an ever-rotating supply, but I always seem to have a hunk of Parmesan or Pecorino, a tub of ricotta, and a bottle of buttermilk. And cheese likes to breathe, so it's best to store your cheese wrapped in parchment paper, not plastic.

HERBS: I get my fresh herbs at a farmers' market. I've found they keep for a week or more with a bit of care. I wash and dry them, then loosely wrap each bundle in a dry paper towel and stack them in a ventilated plastic container.

LEMONS: I pick up two or three lemons every time I shop, ensuring I'm never without one of my most necessary ingredients. There's nothing worse than wanting a hint of acid and finding yourself lemon-less. (Okay, there are many things that are worse, but you know what I mean.)

CONDIMENTS: After years of doing the condiment shuffle in various fridges, I've narrowed it down to my all-star team. These include gochujang, kimchi, red and white miso paste, maple syrup, and lime pickle. It might seem like a confusing mix, but I do recommend them all.

PROTEINS, VEGETABLES, AND THE DAY-TO-DAY: I typically like to source these items a few days before I use them. When my kitchen stockpile is filled and ready, my shopping trips can be quick and agile, with just a couple of small things to pick up.

A FEW TECHNIQUES YOU'LL SEE USED THROUGHOUT THE BOOK

These are not recipes per se, but they are the building blocks for the recipes in this book and well beyond. This is a deeper dive into these skills, to help translate them into your everyday cooking.

BROWNING BUTTER: Browned butter gives a toasty, nutty quality to both sweet and savory foods. Essentially, you're toasting the butter, until 20 percent of its moisture has evaporated and the milk solids begin to brown at the bottom of the pan. Place cubed butter in a small saucepan over medium heat and let it completely melt. (It's important to use stainless steel or light enamel cookware so you can watch the butter; anything with a dark surface will be hard to monitor.) Cook, undisturbed, for 2 to 3 minutes, or until the butter starts to softly foam. Swirl occasionally, watching as the flecks at the bottom of the pan go from lightly golden to rich and dark, 6 to 7 minutes total. Remove the pan from the heat and pour into a bowl to stop the cooking, then use as needed.

BLANCHING NEARLY ANYTHING: Blanching is a gentle cooking method that maintains texture and flavor, locks in nutrition, and instantly brightens produce. I use it most often to save old herbs from the point of extinction and to gently cook vegetables. To blanch anything, bring a large pot of water to a boil and salt it liberally. Prepare a bath of ice water to the side. Boil your ingredients for a few minutes or just until the color is vibrant. Transfer to the ice bath with a spider strainer or sieve. Chill for 2 minutes to cool completely, then they're ready to use. For soft herbs, boil for only 30 to 45 seconds, chill in the ice bath, squeeze out any moisture, and pat completely dry with paper towels.

SHARPENING YOUR KNIVES: There are a variety of options to sharpen knives at home, but I prefer using a whetstone. You can purchase a whetstone online or from a restaurant supply store. Look for one in the $20 to $30 range; you don't need an expensive one. Soak the whetstone in water for 20 to 30 minutes, or until it stops bubbling. Place it on a damp kitchen towel on a flat surface so it won't slip. Starting with the tip of the knife at the top of the stone, slide it along the center of the stone. Keep the knife at a 30 degree angle and use moderate pressure to glide from the tip to the base of the blade, as you go from the top to the bottom of the stone. Flip the knife to do the other side, repeating the process five to eight times per side, and dabbing more water on the whetstone as needed. Wash and dry the knife completely before using.

CHOPPING HERBS, CHIFFONADE AND TORN: A chiffonade cut sounds fancy, because maybe, deep down, we all just want fancy things. Gather a bunch of individual herb leaves, stack them flat so they lay on top of one another, roll the stack into a tight cigar shape, then slice crosswise into thin slivers. When I call for torn herbs, grab a small handful and gently tear them apart. The pieces should be about the size of a lima bean and smell fragrant and amazing.

CUTTING IN BUTTER: For pastry or biscuit dough, you'll need to cut the butter into the flour. There are tools for this, like a pastry blender, but my best tool is my hands, as I like to feel the butter's distribution in the flour. Add cubes of very cold butter to a well of flour. Toss with your fingertips to make sure each piece is coated in flour, then begin pressing the cubes into flat disks, making sure they stay covered in flour. Work in the butter, until the flour mixture is crumbly with big chunks of butter throughout. Because hands naturally radiate heat, start with extra-cold ingredients and work with purpose. Your piecrusts (see page 266) will thank you.

SEASONING TO TASTE: The biggest thing that separates good cooking from great cooking is understanding seasoning. I live by the words: taste, season, adjust, repeat. Most spices and herbs have fat-soluble compounds, which means their flavor really shines when they have brief contact with hot oil. Before adding any liquid, let spices simmer for just a few seconds, until their aroma is powerful. It'll add an incredible layer of flavor. But seasoning can go beyond the typical things and include acid, oil, and hits of umami. A finishing drizzle of a good oil, a squeeze of lemon, a flurry of Parm, some cracks of black pepper, or a sprinkle of flaky salt can be exactly the right touch on the final dish.

STAPLES,
SAUCES &
SMALL RECIPES
TO LIVE BY

MY FAVORITE PART OF COOKBOOKS IS USUALLY THE BEGINNING, where the simplest but most versatile recipes live. I call these "small" recipes, not because they're small in flavor (quite the opposite, actually!), but because they're the small building blocks that consistently live in my kitchen, ready to enhance, support, or supplement everything I cook throughout the week.

In the years I've been cooking, I've been slowly making favorite condiments, toppings, sauces, and sides, finding which ones I return to and stretching them for days of use. I like how these recipes can both add to a meal or end up as the basis of the entire meal itself. I've made more than a dozen dinners of simple fish and roasted vegetables topped with Spinachy Skhug (page 37), and the Salsa Verde (page 36) has seen me through a few too many raw vegetable salads. If I'm in a cooking rut, creamy Tonnato (page 36) reminds me that even with only a few vegetables, I can still make big flavor out of a lackluster fridge (having the sourdough bread crumbs from page 46 ready to go doesn't hurt either).

Many of these recipes draw from cuisines around the world, things I've learned and later obsessed over, which I hope makes their utility that much more exciting as you navigate your way through the recipes in this book. The crux is that each of these recipes becomes what you make of them, so as you cook through them, I hope you will find what fits in your personal kitchen repertoire. I've included as many suggestions as I can for how to use them, but when you discover new ones, please let me know.

YOUR PERFECT HERB OIL

Makes just more than 1 cup

Herb oils never really "worked" for me in my kitchen. While I loved them in restaurants, I felt they were more show than flavor. So I took herb oils into my own hands, creating what isn't exactly an herb oil but a tuned-up homemade version. The vinegar and salt add brightness, making it something versatile enough for a casual drizzle.

USE IT: On soups or salads, spooning it over grilled fish, or dimpling it into focaccia, where it settles into the deep pockets of the bread—which is always supremely satisfying.

> Diamond Crystal kosher salt
>
> 2 cups tender fresh herbs, such as parsley, basil, cilantro, chives
>
> 1½ cups avocado oil
>
> 1 teaspoon champagne vinegar

1. Prepare a large bowl of ice water and set it to the side.

2. Set a large pot over high heat and bring 2 quarts salted water to a boil. Using tongs, submerge the herbs in the boiling water for 30 to 45 seconds. You'll see them start to turn a bright green. Transfer the herbs from the boiling water to the ice bath.

3. When they are cool enough to handle, squeeze out any excess moisture and add the herbs and avocado oil to a blender. Blend until very smooth; this takes me 1 to 3 minutes. Strain through a fine-mesh sieve into a bowl, using a spoon to press out as much liquid green as possible. Whisk in the vinegar and ½ teaspoon salt. Store in the fridge for up to 2 weeks.

NOTE: Play around with the leafy tender herbs, from parsley to dill to tarragon or even a mix. Plus, if you're looking at a batch of herbs close to wilting in your fridge, this is a perfect way to use them.

SHIMMERY, PEPPERY HOT SAUCE

Makes ½ cup

This is nowhere close to bottled hot sauce, and that's no shade to bottled hot sauce (Frank's, *I love you*). This is a chunky, drippy combo of Fresno peppers, habaneros, and shallots that's *just* the right ratio of sweet to spicy. No blending (or, god forbid, fermenting) is required; it all happens in under 10 minutes. Keep the seeds in the peppers if you like extra heat, but I opt to remove them so I can serve this shiny, glisteny sauce by the spoonful.

USE IT: While it can keep in your fridge for days, I love it when it's still warm, especially with pan-fried fish, over grilled veggies, or alongside Tofu Cutlets (page 213).

> 1 tablespoon plus 2 teaspoons apple cider vinegar
>
> 1 tablespoon plus 2 teaspoons honey
>
> Extra-virgin olive oil
>
> 2 small shallots, minced
>
> 2 habanero peppers, seeded and finely chopped
>
> 2 Fresno peppers, seeded and finely chopped
>
> Diamond Crystal kosher salt
>
> 2 garlic cloves, grated

1. In a small bowl, whisk together the vinegar and honey and set aside.

2. Set a small saucepan over medium heat and add 2 tablespoons olive oil. Add the shallots, habaneros, and Fresnos and cook, stirring occasionally, until the peppers have softened and the shallots are translucent, 4 to 5 minutes.

3. Season with a pinch of salt, then add the garlic and cook for an additional 1 to 2 minutes, until the garlic is softened and fragrant. Turn the heat to low and add the vinegar and honey mixture. Give everything a final swirl in the pan and cook for another minute.

4. Remove from the heat and allow it to cool before tasting and adjusting the seasoning. Once cool, transfer to a container and store in the fridge for up to 2 weeks.

YOUR PERFECT HERB OIL

SHIMMERY, PEPPERY HOT SAUCE

SALSA VERDE WITH PRESERVED LEMON

TONNATO

SALSA VERDE WITH PRESERVED LEMON

Makes 1 cup

One of my favorite salsa verdes is the Italian version, which typically contains parsley, shallots, capers, lemon, and olive oil. Here I use preserved lemon to add an even brinier, tangier note. It's all about the search for the right ratio of ingredients, with elements falling into place when the acid meets the saltiness, and everything is tempered by the freshness of the herbs. It should be a balance of bright, acidic, and salty that hits your taste buds in a punchy, vibrant way.

This sauce was formative in my cooking education for teaching me about seasoning because you must constantly taste it to get it right. Taste, season, adjust, and repeat.

1 small shallot, minced

1 tablespoon nonpareil capers, finely chopped

½ preserved lemon, homemade (see page 39) or store-bought (such as Mina), seeded and very finely chopped

2 cups fresh parsley leaves, finely chopped

3 tablespoons fresh lemon juice (about 1 lemon), plus more as needed

¼ teaspoon red pepper flakes

Extra-virgin olive oil

Diamond Crystal kosher salt

Freshly ground black pepper

In a small bowl, combine the shallot, capers, preserved lemon, parsley, lemon juice, pepper flakes, and ⅔ cup olive oil and mix. Season with ¼ teaspoon salt and ¼ teaspoon black pepper. Adjust with more oil or lemon juice and salt and black pepper to taste.

NOTE: Once you graduate from Salsa Verde University (which I just founded here on my couch), there's room to mix and match. Add chopped pieces of any crispy, crunchy vegetable. I love tossing in some thinly sliced radishes, a handful of dill, or a vegetable I have overstocked in my fridge. Salsa verde is one big dressing, and it's happy to welcome other ingredients into the mix.

TONNATO

Makes 1½ cups

Tonnato is an Italian tuna-based sauce, but even for the tuna skeptics among us, this zippy, salty, creamy dressing is worth a try. I take a slight detour from the classic version, swapping the key element of mayonnaise for cashew cream; that omission cuts out the heaviness from this already creamy sauce, brightens the profile, and still carries through the same emulsion.

USE IT: Tonnato is drizzly in the best possible way. Put it on salads, swipe grilled summer vegetables through it, or swirl it into beans. There's also my favorite option: straight off the spoon.

½ cup raw cashews

1 cup boiling water, plus more as needed

1 (5-ounce) can tuna, packed in oil

6 flat anchovy fillets, packed in oil

1 garlic clove

¼ teaspoon red pepper flakes

1 tablespoon fresh lemon juice (about ½ lemon)

Freshly ground black pepper

⅓ cup cold water

Diamond Crystal kosher salt

1. In a small heatproof bowl, combine the cashews and boiling water, ensuring there's enough to fully cover them. Let the cashews sit for 10 minutes.

2. In a blender, combine the tuna (oil and all), anchovy fillets, garlic, pepper flakes, lemon juice, and a few cracks of black pepper. Drain the cashews and add them to the blender with the cold water. Blend everything together until it's very smooth, 2 to 3 minutes. Taste and season with salt and more black pepper as needed.

NOTE: Half the fun of tonnato is treating it like a grown-up tuna salad—in sauce form. There are two variations I love to play around with: For a brighter flavor, I make an herby tonnato with a handful of dill (no stems) thrown in. When I'm craving some heat, I add a tablespoon of Calabrian chili paste, but any hot sauce will work.

SPINACHY SKHUG

Makes 1½ cups

I first had this Yemeni hot sauce slathered on a plate of hot yuca fries at a small window-only take-out spot in Bushwick. I know the fries probably helped, but that sauce made an impression on me, and I've made many pilgrimages back ever since. *Skhug* derives from a Yemeni Arabic word meaning "to crush," but I've taken some poetic license to translate that as "to blend." It's a spicy, herby, verdant sauce, but I've added spinach and a handful of almonds to make the sauce a bit thicker and greener, while keeping its signature heat and brightness.

USE IT: On any sandwich or grain bowl, swiped under beans (see page 164), in salads, or alongside roasted vegetables.

 2 cups fresh cilantro leaves

 1 cup baby spinach

 2 tablespoons raw almonds

 2 jalapeños, seeded

 1 teaspoon ground coriander

 1 teaspoon ground cumin

 Extra-virgin olive oil

 3 tablespoons fresh lemon juice (about 1 lemon)

 Diamond Crystal kosher salt

In a blender, combine the cilantro, spinach, almonds, jalapeños, coriander, and cumin. Pour in ¾ cup olive oil and the lemon juice and add ¼ teaspoon salt. Blend until smooth. Taste and adjust the seasoning as needed. Store in the fridge for up to 1 week.

CHARRED-TOMATO DRESSING

Makes 2 cups

Somewhere between a salsa, dressing, and gazpacho, this tangy roasted tomato sauce is having a *slight* identity crisis. But the identity crisis is what makes it one of my most versatile favorites. It's best used after giving the charred tomatoes a few minutes to sit and meld with the other ingredients, and I'll always say it's the most satisfying thing to watch the bright pools of olive oil gather at the top and shatter as you mix.

USE IT: Add it to eggs and dips and drag focaccia through it, pile it on top of thick swordfish fillets, or toss it over some buttered rice.

 3 globe tomatoes, various colors (or Roma, tomatoes on the vine, or beefsteak)

 2 tablespoons red wine vinegar, plus more to taste

 2 garlic cloves, grated

 ½ teaspoon red pepper flakes

 Diamond Crystal kosher salt

 Freshly ground black pepper

 Extra-virgin olive oil

1. Position a rack in the center of the oven and set the broiler to high.

2. Place the tomatoes on a sheet pan and broil until the skin is charred and peeling, about 10 minutes. Broilers can be incredibly fickle, so start checking for char marks after 5 minutes. Flip and char the other side, until the tomatoes are soft and begin to release some of their juices, 5 to 7 minutes. Remove and set aside.

3. Once the tomatoes are cool enough to handle, coarsely chop them into small pieces. In a medium bowl, combine the tomatoes, their juices, the vinegar and garlic. Season with the pepper flakes, ½ teaspoon salt, and ¼ teaspoon black pepper. Add 3 tablespoons olive oil and stir. Taste and adjust with more salt, black pepper, and oil as needed.

SPINACHY SKHUG

CHARRED-TOMATO DRESSING

CASHEW CREAM

(QUICKER) PRESERVED LEMONS

CASHEW CREAM OR ANY NUT-BASED CREAM FOR THAT MATTER

Makes a little over 1 cup

Nuts plus water equal creamy, and I truly don't think we talk about it enough. There's something wonderfully unique about a plant-based cream, which adds a subtly rich flavor that always gets along with vegetables, breads, and most proteins. The formula is about the same for every nut, but I'm partial to cashews, walnuts, almonds, and pecans because of their smoother texture and quick blending process.

USE IT: As you would sour cream or yogurt to add creaminess wherever it's needed (or just wanted), for garnishing soups, swiped on bread, or spread under roasted potatoes. Thin it with cool water to use as a substitute for heavy cream or leave it as is and use it in place of ricotta.

> 1 cup cashews
>
> 2 cups boiling water
>
> 2 teaspoons fresh lemon juice (just a big squeeze)
>
> Diamond Crystal kosher salt
>
> Freshly ground black pepper

1. In a heatproof medium bowl, add the cashews and cover them with the boiling water. Let them soak for 15 minutes but the longer, the better, up to 1 hour.

2. Drain the water from the nuts and place them in a blender. Add ⅔ cup cool water, the lemon juice, ½ teaspoon salt, and a few cracks of black pepper. Blend until smooth. Add more cool water, a tablespoon at a time, as needed to get to your preferred thickness. Taste and season with salt to taste. Store in the fridge for up to 2 weeks.

(QUICKER) PRESERVED LEMONS

Makes two 16-ounce mason jars

In my daily life, I use a lot of lemons, and I mean *a lot of lemons.* And throwing out all those perfectly good lemon rinds? Criminal. I had been wanting to find a different (read: quicker) way to make preserved lemons for a while, and an abundance of peels led me to a shortcut version that creates the same briny, salty, acidic hit that a preserved lemon gives you, without waiting a month. This recipe does require some new lemons ready for juicing, but it makes enough brine to cover your used lemon-peel soldiers, too. Even the discarded lemon halves provide a good hit of flavor to the brine, so it feels like teamwork. Plus you only have to wait 7 days for these to be ready, which to me feels like a bargain.

> 4 whole lemons
>
> 2 leftover previously squeezed lemons (4 halves, in my case)
>
> Diamond Crystal kosher salt
>
> 1 whole clove

1. Wash the whole lemons well and cut them in half. Juice the lemons and set the spent rinds aside (they should yield about ⅔ cup juice, but it doesn't have to be perfect). If you have less than ½ cup, juice another lemon to get to that amount.

2. Set a medium pot over high heat and bring 2 quarts water to a boil. Add all the lemon halves and boil for 10 minutes to soften the rinds. Turn down the heat to keep the pot from boiling over.

3. Scoop the lemons out of the water and divide them between two jars. It should be a snug fit.

4. Return the water to a soft boil and add the lemon juice, ⅓ cup salt, and the clove. Let this boil until the salt dissolves. Turn off the heat and pour the brine over the lemons. Let the jars cool to room temperature before sealing and storing.

5. Store in the fridge for at least 1 week before using, flipping the jars to rest upside down every few days to prevent the salt from settling. When they're ready, the lemons will function and taste exactly like preserved lemons. Store in the fridge for up to 1 month after they're ready for use.

CRUMBLED CHICKPEAS

Makes 1½ cups

It was at a neighborhood spot, The James (I miss you!), where I fell in love with crispy chickpeas: a full-fat, full-fried 'pea, scattered with pieces of rosemary and a lot of salt. I stated to my dinner partner multiple times, "I could eat these on everything," and after saying something enough, it undoubtedly leads you to trying it. And that's how whole 'peas turned to crumbled 'peas. Briefly pulsed in a food processor and then doused in olive oil, these crumbled chickpeas still get frizzly at the edges and when done right, can be used to garnish salads, grain bowls, avocado toasts, curries, or anywhere you'd want a bread crumb. For best results, add your favorite spices (we're using za'atar here) and note that a little can go a long way.

1 (15-ounce) can chickpeas, drained and rinsed

Extra-virgin olive oil

1 tablespoon za'atar

Diamond Crystal kosher salt

1 . Position a rack in the top third of the oven and preheat it to 400°F. Line a sheet pan with parchment paper.

2 . Dry the chickpeas well before adding them to a food processor. Pulse until they resemble coarsely ground bread crumbs, loosening them with a fork as necessary so you don't form a paste. Spread these out evenly on the lined sheet pan and drizzle all over with 3 tablespoons olive oil (you want them pretty covered). Season with the za'atar and ½ teaspoon salt. Gently mix until everything is evenly coated.

3 . Roast the chickpeas until they are golden and dry, 20 to 25 minutes, shaking and stirring with a spatula halfway through to help them crisp up.

CRISPY, CRAGGILY CROUTONS

Makes 2 cups

It takes all my willpower to remind myself that this is an accompaniment to salads and soups and not just a snack for me to eat straight off the pan. And I'm going to be picky here and ask that you please, *please* make these with either tangy, crusty sourdough or fluffy, fresh brioche. And you do want fresh bread—day-old bread makes an almost rocklike crouton. The method is the same for both breads, but the results will be quite different: The sourdough will have a chewier, crunchier texture, good for absorbing sauces and soaking up soups, while the brioche will have a tender crispness, perfect for delicate salads or lighter recipes. These croutons will last about 7 days in an airtight container in a cool, dry place but will probably be gone long before then.

3 thick slices sourdough or fresh brioche

Extra-virgin olive oil

Flaky salt

1 . Position a rack in the center of the oven and preheat it to 375°F.

2 . Gently tear the bread into rough, uneven pieces, the more jagged edges, the better. Spread the bread on a large sheet pan and drizzle with 2 tablespoons olive oil. Toss to coat, then sprinkle with 1 teaspoon salt.

3 . Bake until the croutons are evenly golden and crisp, 15 to 18 minutes, shaking and tossing halfway through.

NOTE: Salt the croutons before baking, never after, due to what I call the "cling factor." Salting before lets the salt cling to the finished result, leaving you big crystals of salt hidden across the olive oil–coated bread. And nothing beats biting into a big pocket of salt on a crispy crouton. There's some giant pretzel energy there that I want to relive every day.

CRUMBLED CHICKPEAS

CRISPY, CRAGGILY CROUTONS

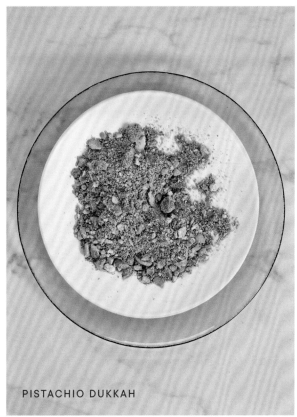

PISTACHIO DUKKAH

SAVORY SEED SPRINKLE

PISTACHIO DUKKAH

Makes 1½ cups

Dukkah, or do'a, was the most memorable food gift I've ever received. A mix of toasty nuts and seeds, dukkah is common in the Middle East and North Africa. The person who gifted it told me that in Egypt you can tell a family by the smell of the dukkah recipe wafting from their home. And in that way, I'm grateful to my friend for welcoming me into her home by sharing hers, and I hope to carry through the same respect for the recipe with this version.

USE IT: Sprinkle it on eggs, a savory yogurt bowl, a salad, or grilled vegetables for a nutty, savory crunch.

⅓ cup pistachios

¼ cup raw almonds

2 tablespoons fennel seeds

2 tablespoons coriander seeds

2 tablespoons cumin seeds

2 tablespoons white sesame seeds

Diamond Crystal kosher salt

¼ teaspoon cayenne pepper

1. Set a large pan over medium heat and add the pistachios and almonds. Toast, stirring occasionally, until the almonds are a shade darker and the pistachios are fragrant, 4 to 5 minutes. Transfer these to a large bowl.

2. Add the fennel seeds to the pan and toast until fragrant, 2 to 3 minutes. Add them to the same bowl. Repeat this process with all the remaining seeds. The coriander and cumin seeds will toast in 2 to 3 minutes, while the sesame seeds will take 6 to 7 minutes to get golden. The pan may smoke a bit from the fat it picked up from the nuts and seeds but don't mind it.

3. Add all the toasted seeds to the bowl with the nuts and let them cool for 1 to 2 minutes. Transfer to a food processor. Pulse until the mix is coarsely ground but not yet fine, 15 to 30 seconds. It should resemble the texture of coarse sand.

4. Return the mixture to the bowl, season with 1 teaspoon salt and the cayenne, and mix to combine. Taste and add more salt as needed. Store in a jar in a cool, dry place for up to 2 months.

SAVORY SEED SPRINKLE

Makes ½ cup

Half a hybrid version of everything-but-the-bagel seasoning and half a younger sister of za'atar, this is an all-purpose savory seed sprinkle to put on nearly, well, everything. The secret of this sprinkle's deliciousness is how it is lightly toasted in sesame oil, a step that might not seem necessary until you taste how savory and nutty it can become. It's filled with all the good stuff that I want to be eating, even if it's just an excuse to be simultaneously inhaling minced onion pieces.

USE IT: On eggs, with avocado toast, baked on top of your favorite whole wheat loaf, or on any salad or soup that could use a little crunch.

1 tablespoon sunflower seeds

1 tablespoon hemp hearts

1 tablespoon flaxseeds or flaxseed meal

1 tablespoon white sesame seeds

1 tablespoon dried oregano

1 tablespoon dried minced onion

1 teaspoon red pepper flakes

1 teaspoon ground sumac

1 teaspoon toasted sesame oil

Flaky salt

1. Using a mortar and pestle, crush the sunflower seeds finely, until they are about one-quarter of their original size and the texture of coarse bread crumbs.

2. In a medium bowl, combine the ground sunflower seeds, hemp hearts, flaxseeds, sesame seeds, oregano, dried minced onion, pepper flakes, and sumac.

3. Set a small stainless steel pan over medium heat and add the sesame oil. Let this heat up until fragrant, a minute or so. Add the seed mixture and cook until the seeds begin to smell nutty and the sesame is golden brown, 2 to 3 minutes.

4. Transfer to a bowl and add 1 teaspoon salt. Funnel it into a jar, cover, and keep it in a cool, dry place for up to 1 month.

CRISPY QUINOA

Makes ¾ cup

Born as an attempt to make quinoa less, well . . . "*quinoa*," I decided to see what would happen if I toasted this tiny, fluffy grain. After a successful trial in the oven, this crispy quinoa ended up on my favorite kale salad, and I've never looked back. It has become one of my most versatile toppings, showing up over salads (see Baked Kale Salad with Chili Quinoa, page 113), beneath scallops (see Smoky Scallops over Crispy Quinoa, page 221), scattered on dips, and stirred into soups. This quinoa is highly adaptable, can go with (almost) everything, and keeps its crisp for up to 2 weeks (you read that right). One of my recipe testers shared that she puts it in jars and gives it as gifts, and that, to me, is the highest honor this protein-packed grain can receive.

The best part of this recipe is in the extras. You can build flavor in crispy quinoa both through the oil you toss it in and the "finishers" you add in the last 10 minutes. See the lists for some of my favorites.

1 cup quinoa, any kind

Extra-virgin olive oil or oil of choice (see list below)

Diamond Crystal kosher salt

1 tablespoon finisher of choice (see list below); optional

1. Cook the quinoa according to the package directions and set aside.

2. Position a rack in the top of the oven and preheat it to 375°F. Line a sheet pan with parchment paper.

3. Spread the quinoa evenly in a single layer on the lined sheet pan, with no pieces on top of each other. Drizzle with 2 tablespoons olive oil and season with ¼ teaspoon salt. Mix to coat.

4. Bake for 25 to 30 minutes, stirring halfway through. If using a finisher, add it after 15 minutes of baking and use a spatula to mix it in. Continue baking until the quinoa is golden brown, shrunken, and crispy.

OILS OR FATS (CHOOSE 1)		FINISHERS (CHOOSE 1)	
Sesame oil	Brown butter (see page 30)	Balsamic glaze	Hot sauce, such as sriracha or Tabasco
Chili oil		Hot honey	
	Walnut oil	Soy sauce	Agave syrup
Your Perfect Herb Oil (page 34)	Infused olive oils, such as rosemary oil	Lemon juice	Calabrian chili paste
		Sherry vinegar	

ROASTED GARLIC WITH FLAKY SALT

Makes 2 garlic bulbs

AKA how I turn garlic cloves into straight spreadable heaven. If you aren't serving this with bread, these cloves are still great to use in place of raw garlic for a less sharp but nice and toasty addition to pastas, salad dressings, spreads, and soups.

2 garlic bulbs

Extra-virgin olive oil

Flaky salt

1. Position a rack in the center of the oven and preheat it to 400°F.

2. Slice off the top third of the garlic bulbs and cover each with ½ tablespoon olive oil, letting it soak into the crevices between the cloves. Wrap the bulbs in aluminum foil or add them to a small clay garlic roaster with a lid and roast until the garlic is golden brown, sticky on top, and softened throughout, 40 to 45 minutes.

3. Scatter ¼ teaspoon flaky salt over the top of each bulb before using or serving.

A SINGLE-PURPOSE GARLIC ROASTER

I don't often advocate for niche kitchen tools, but that rule does not extend to my dad's clay garlic roaster, which I'll probably be endeared to for the rest of my life. Back then, I only ever saw it used on the rare occasion when my dad would take a garlic head, slice off the top, douse it in olive oil, and roast it—taking up what was probably *very valuable* real estate in our oven during holidays. Everyone was expected to dip a knife directly into the garlic head, pull out their personal clove, and spread it on the crustiest of bread with a scoop of butter and a sprinkle of table salt, straight from the shaker. In my world now, there are more kinds of salt (and bread—I like More Butter Than Rolls on page 238 with this), but there's still only one way I want to roast garlic.

SOURDOUGH BREAD CRUMBS, THE BIGGER KIND

Makes just more than 2 cups

You'll see bread crumbs far and wide throughout this book, and that's because they are, simply put, a perfect topping. Pulling out my food processor to blitz up some old sourdough is always worth it, and while croutons are better made with fresh bread, I like day-old sourdough for these. They tend to be bigger, grainier, soak up sauces better than store-bought crumbs, and have a subtle sour tang. You can see them on eggs (see Kimchi-Crusted Poached Eggs, page 78), all over my favorite vegetables (Greener Zucchini Gratin, page 143), and even on top of bread (see Drippy Harissa Eggplant, page 94), which yes, feels like doubling up, but when it comes to bread, why wouldn't you?

6 to 8 slices day-old sourdough bread (10 ounces)

Extra-virgin olive oil

Diamond Crystal kosher salt

NOTE: With bread crumbs, there's always room to layer flavor. For smokier bread crumbs, I add ¼ teaspoon smoked paprika per 1 cup crumbs. You can also swap in a chili oil for the olive oil or use brown butter instead of oil for an extra-toasty crumb.

1. Position a rack in the center of the oven and preheat it to 350°F.

2. Tear the bread into big chunks and spread the chunks on a sheet pan. Bake for 9 to 12 minutes to get the bread dry but not golden.

3. Let it cool, then add the bread to a food processor and process until all the pieces are smaller than a lentil. Some pieces will be bigger and smaller than others, but that's totally okay.

4. These crumbs can be stored in an airtight bag in the fridge for up to 2 weeks.

5. If you plan to use them right away, either prepare them according to your recipe's instructions or use the following method: Place a medium pan over medium heat and add 1 tablespoon olive oil per 1 cup bread crumbs. Add the bread crumbs to the pan, season with a few pinches of salt, and toast for 3 to 4 minutes, stirring occasionally, until the bread crumbs are a deep golden. Remove from the pan and use as preferred.

FAROFA

Makes 2 cups

Farofa reminds me of a coffee cake crumble topping—gone savory. It's a Brazilian staple made from cassava flour, although this recipe adds chickpea flour for some additional protein and texture. The flours are toasted softly with butter, red onion, and smoked paprika, and I toss in some fried garlic at the end for an additional layer of crunch. It's traditionally a side dish, but I love to top stews, soups, and bean-y things with it; ergo, giving almost anything a salty, garlicky crumbly crust.

Extra-virgin olive oil

4 garlic cloves, thinly sliced crosswise

4 tablespoons salted butter

1 small red onion, diced

Diamond Crystal kosher salt

½ cup cassava flour

½ cup chickpea flour

½ teaspoon smoked paprika

Freshly ground black pepper

1. Set a large pan over medium heat and add 2 tablespoons olive oil. Let it heat up for a minute; it's ready when you add a slice of garlic and it softly sizzles. Pan-fry the garlic slices, until both sides are golden brown, 3 to 4 minutes, flipping after 2 minutes. They can go from golden to burnt in seconds, so keep an eye on them. Remove the garlic from the pan, coarsely chop, and set the garlic chips aside.

2. In the same pan, melt 2 tablespoons of the butter. Turn the heat to medium-low, add the red onion, and season with salt. Cook, stirring occasionally, until the onion is softened and noticeably darker in color, 12 to 13 minutes.

3. Add the cassava flour, chickpea flour, smoked paprika, and the remaining 2 tablespoons butter. As the butter melts, the flour will clump into big pieces. Continue to stir as the butter melts fully and use a spatula to encourage everything to form a big, savory crumble. Taste, season with salt and black pepper, and continue to cook until the flour turns from white to a slightly orangey yellow, another 3 to 4 minutes.

4. Scrape the mixture into a large bowl, add the garlic chips, and give one last mix to combine. Either eat right away or store in an airtight container in the fridge for up to 1 week.

HOW TO QUICK PICKLE ANYTHING

Makes enough brine for two 16-ounce mason jars of pickled vegetables

In my kitchen, all my pickles are quick pickles. That's because (1) I am not a professional fermenter and don't want to accidentally kill someone, and (2) even quick pickles grow in flavor over time. A pickled radish might (and does!) have a completely different flavor and color on day 3 than day 10, and the only way to find out your favorite day is to start pickling.

In my trials, I've concluded (maybe unpopularly) that sweet brines and salt brines are equally important. And while I don't commit to the common 1:1:1 ratio (you can get a similar at-home pickle using way fewer ingredients), both my salt brine and a sweeter version below work for almost any vegetable your heart desires. I have a few suggested guidelines in the chart on page 50, but that's just what they are: suggestions. Play around with your vegetables, do some damage at a farmers' market, quickly pickle everything, and call me when you've figured out what day your radishes taste best (I'm going to give you a solid prediction for day 6).

¾ cup distilled white vinegar

¾ cup water

Diamond Crystal kosher salt

2 tablespoons sugar (optional, for a sweeter variation)

NOTE: Storage times vary, but out of an abundance of caution, store these pickles in the fridge for no more than 1 month.

1. Set a small pot over medium-high heat and add the vinegar, water, 1 tablespoon salt, and the sugar (if using). Bring the mixture to a gentle simmer, stirring until everything has dissolved.

2. Add the vegetables/fruits and flavor additions of choice to two jars and pour the brine over the top. Place a lid on top but don't seal until the brine has completely cooled to room temperature, then screw on the top and move it to the refrigerator.

Recipe and ingredients continue

VEGETABLE/FRUIT	CUT	BRINE	ADDITIONS
Cucumbers, any variety	Quartered, lengthwise	Salt	Fresh dill, black peppercorns, fennel seeds, caraway seeds
Radishes, carrots, parsnips, beets, other root vegetables	Sliced or halved	Salt or sweet	Black peppercorns, coriander seeds, bay leaf
Fennel, Brussels sprouts, cabbage	Shaved or chopped	Salt	Bay leaf, mustard seeds, fennel seeds, caraway seeds
Cherries, grapes, peaches, plums	Sliced or halved	Sweet	Cloves, star anise, allspice berries, cinnamon stick
Red onions, rhubarb, ginger	Thinly sliced or shaved	Sweet	Black peppercorns, cloves, bay leaf
Hot peppers and sweet peppers	Sliced or halved	Salt	Mustard seeds, celery seeds, bay leaf
Onions, ramps, shallots, scallions	Thinly sliced or halved	Salt	Black peppercorns, mustard seeds, celery seeds
Summer squash, zucchini, pattypans	Thinly sliced into medallions or long strips with a vegetable peeler	Salt	Fresh dill, red pepper flakes, fenugreek seeds, celery seeds, dill seeds

SNACKS
ARE ALWAYS
MORE THAN
SNACKS

AT PRESENT TIME, THERE ARE 287 KINDS OF LAY'S POTATO CHIP FLAVORS IN THE WORLD, excluding limited editions. It's fair to assume we are a culture of snacks.

Now I'm not going to give you a chapter of homemade potato chip recipes, since my pride can admit the packaged guys just do it better. But if I am going to give you a chapter about snacks (which, hello, we are here), I want to give you the snacks that can also flex to be a little bit more than snacks—because we've already nailed the recipe for cheese and crackers.

The snacks in this chapter stretch from filling and quick, to what I call sweatpants snacks (see the popcorn on page 61, which fulfills all my snacks-in-pajamas dreams), all the way to big and communal. But the goal was to make sure each of these recipes has a high utility—that they aren't just afterthoughts in your kitchen but a good reason to make a snack. A snack worth cooking for.

When I think of their usefulness, I think both in terms of taste and the time they take to prepare. Some snacks might take a bit more effort (see the Figs in a Blanket, page 58, for a fun time), then there are faster snacks you can batch-make for the entire week (see A Trio of Dips, page 67) and the two-second snack, for when your fridge is sparse and hunger levels are code-red (see the Jammy Eggs Three Ways on page 54).

And while all the snacks in this chapter are vastly different (if Lay's has 287 variations, I can at least give you 7!), one thing stays the same: These snacks balance between filling, useful, and fun. Because that's what a good snack is—something that is always a bit more than what you'd expect.

JAMMY EGGS THREE WAYS

A halved jammy egg is my "any time of day" snack. There are approximately eight million (give or take) ways to make a jammy egg a flavor bomb, with a few hits of vinegar here, a touch of herbs there, or a fillet of anchovy or two. It's all about building the right layers of flavor, with ingredients that will only take you seconds to pull out. Quick, simple, snackable. And just a little bit messy.

HOW TO MAKE JAMMY EGGS

1. Prepare an ice water bath and set it to the side of your stove.

2. Set a medium pot of water over high heat and bring it to a rolling boil. Gently lower in the eggs and let them boil for 6 to 7 minutes. I've found 6½ on the nose is my sweet spot for easy-to-peel eggs with a perfectly molten center. Use a slotted spoon to lift the eggs from the pot and gently drop them into the ice bath. I've also been known to keep them in the slotted spoon and just run cool water over them from the tap. They're easiest to peel when they've just cooled, but you can also store them in their shells in the fridge to crack and eat at any time.

NOTE: I have three styles of my ideal jammy-egg snack, each hitting a different spot, but they all follow the same loose formula: There's a hint of acid to play off the yolk, a few aromatics, and a big hit of salt. The yolk is so fatty that I don't always put an oil or fat with these, but there are some exceptions, which the following chart lays out.

	HOT & VINEGARY	DILLY WITH ANCHOVY	SMOKY & BREADCRUMBY
AN ACID	Add less than ½ teaspoon of red wine vinegar to the center yolk.	Grab a lemon wedge and squeeze it over.	Sprinkle ½ teaspoon of red wine vinegar over the yolk.
AROMATICS	Dot on a few drops of your favorite hot sauce (I live and die for Frank's RedHot).	Top with a few torn pieces of dill (chives are also welcome).	Add a hefty pinch of paprika to 2 to 3 tablespoons of bread crumbs (page 46).
A SALTY THING	Sprinkle with flaky salt. Bonus points for a few hits of black pepper.	Season the herbs with the smallest pinch of kosher salt, place them on the egg, and top with a flat anchovy fillet.	Season the bread crumb mixture with kosher salt.
A FAT		Drizzle some basil oil (see Your Perfect Herb Oil, page 34) on top for a nice color.	Add the bread crumbs to a medium pan over medium heat with a drizzle of olive oil. Toast for 1 to 2 minutes. Serve piled over the eggs.

HOT & VINEGARY

SMOKY &
BREADCRUMBY

DILLY WITH ANCHOVY

FIGS THAT SPEAK

The first farmers' market I ever went to was the Santa Monica farmers' market, which, for context, is like someone who's only seen football once walking into the Super Bowl. It. Was. Massive. And I was instantly lost. This was also the point in my life when I thought farmers' markets were for picking up a fun candle and a baguette to match your aesthetic. I didn't buy into the idea that people actually *grocery shopped* there. Years later, I've had the opportunity (both financially and with my time) to support many markets of varying size and intensity, but Santa Monica's will always trump them all.

Twenty-year-old me navigated through crowds of shoppers and miles of vendors. I walked past mountains of California citrus, piles of avocados, stalls and stalls of tomatoes, and one small tent selling figs. I had only seen figs in movies before.

"One box of figs, please."

"Okay! Which one speaks to you?"

"Speaks to me?"

(It did not feel like any were speaking to me.)

"Ummmm these ones."

I chose a box with one big fig and many baby figs.

"Amazing! Enjoy! Treat them well!"

Five dollars: gone. Figs that spoke—acquired.

I left that market overwhelmed and overly excited. The figs ended up being fine. Not every fruit is going to be magic.

But even past all their "fine"-ness, the experience stayed with me. These were my gateway figs.

I didn't become a farmers' market devotee all at once; my appreciation grew over time. With each trip, I learned more, tasted more: discovering how much better late-summer zucchini are, tasting a butternut squash so sweet you could eat it thinly shaved and raw, or seeing how long basil can last when you buy it straight from the source—these were all lessons I picked up as I continued to come back to markets, and it made me a better cook. The figs were what brought me back for my second time, but a vendor I met then was the one who brought me back for my third, and building a meal around my finds is what brought me back for my fourth. And it just kept going. Turns out, local veg can be a pretty addicting thing.

So, now I speak to farmers (not figs, surprisingly), who help me pick out the best items of the season and share what they're harvesting next. Past their recommendations, I've come to trust my cravings and my eyes. And in times where I carry a bit too much home from a produce haul, I always justify it with the argument: "I don't know—it spoke to me."

FIGS IN A BLANKET

Makes 16 tucked-in figs

Figs in a blanket are the sweeter and well-deserving vegetarian counterpart to pigs in a blanket that seem to get all "snack-in-blanket" glory. The pastry fold is different, since figs have a different shape than tiny hot dogs, but the concept is the same—one delicious thing packaged inside another delicious thing. I love making these with peak-season summer figs, but if you're in a pinch, dried figs work, too; just keep them whole instead of halving them.

1 tablespoon honey

1 tablespoon red wine vinegar

Diamond Crystal kosher salt

Freshly ground black pepper

8 small fresh figs

2 tablespoons pistachios, very finely chopped

1 tablespoon white sesame seeds

Rye Pastry Dough (page 266)

1 large egg, beaten

NOTE: For a sweet and savory combo, I've swapped the pistachio-sesame mixture for an equal amount of the Pistachio Dukkah (page 42), and it's always a wild crowd pleaser.

1. Position a rack in the center of the oven and preheat it to 375°F. Line a sheet pan with parchment paper.

2. In a medium bowl, whisk together the honey, vinegar, ¼ teaspoon salt, and a few cracks of black pepper. Remove the tips from the figs, halve them lengthwise, and add them to the bowl. Toss to coat them in the vinegar and set aside.

3. In a small bowl, stir together the pistachios and sesame seeds.

4. On a lightly floured surface, roll out the pastry dough into a 12-inch square. Cut the dough into four columns lengthwise and four columns crosswise, creating sixteen 3-inch squares of dough.

5. Place one fig piece in the center of each dough square but don't discard the fig marinade. Fold up two opposite corners of the dough to pinch in the center, then fold up the bottom corner, encasing the fig and creating the "fig in a blanket." Do this with all sixteen pieces and place them evenly spaced out on the lined sheet pan.

6. Add the egg to the leftover fig marinade and whisk to create an egg wash. Brush each pastry with the egg wash and liberally sprinkle both the pastry and figs with the pistachio-sesame mixture.

7. Bake until golden, 25 to 30 minutes. Serve warm.

TURMERIC POPCORN & CROUTONS

Makes 12 cups

As a self-proclaimed "texture person," I always thought popcorn was a perfect snack, but then croutons entered the picture. This bowl is two types of crunch in one, with a pile of textures and a movie-theater-butter yellow glow from a spicy, coconutty turmeric oil. While the process might feel very popcorn 2.0, the steps are streamlined to one pot, making this a great sweatpants popcorn but equally worthy of serving at your next party. Just make sure to have plenty of napkins on hand, because popcorn 2.0 doesn't play nicely with clean fingers.

5 tablespoons coconut oil, melted

2 slices sourdough bread, torn into big chunks

½ cup popcorn kernels

1 tablespoon ground turmeric

1 teaspoon sambal oelek or sriracha

Diamond Crystal kosher salt

Freshly ground black pepper

1. Set a large pot with a tight-fitting lid over medium-high heat and add 2 tablespoons of the coconut oil. Let it heat up for about 1 minute or until you can smell a bit of the coconutty aroma. Add the bread chunks and give the pot a quick shake to coat the bread in oil. Cook until the bread is golden brown on one side, about 2 minutes, then flip the pieces and toast for an additional 2 minutes. Remove the croutons from the pot.

2. Add another tablespoon of the coconut oil to the pan. Turn the heat to medium, add 2 or 3 kernels of popcorn to the pan, and cover. When you hear the first kernels pop, add the rest of the kernels and cover with a lid. Let the popcorn do its thing, popping for 3 to 5 minutes.

3. While the kernels are popping, whisk together the remaining 2 tablespoons coconut oil with the turmeric, sambal oelek, and ½ teaspoon salt.

4. When the popcorn has finished popping, remove the pan from the heat and toss in the croutons, drizzle the turmeric oil over the top, and add a few cracks of black pepper. Cover the pan again and give everything a quick shake to coat.

5. Pour everything into a big bowl, season with more salt and black pepper as needed, and crunch.

LEMON, ALMOND & GARLIC CHIPS

Makes 2 cups

If I could buy garlic chips by the bag, I would. I still think it's a crime that we can't, although I'm sure in grocery stores much more equipped than mine, there is that option. This is a nut mix that gives the people (me) what they really want: fried garlic chips, crunchy almonds, light and crispy buckwheat groats, and a good squeeze of lemon. If you don't have almonds, don't worry, the three levels of crunch will stay no matter what nut you use. Save the squeeze of lemon for the end; otherwise, you run the risk of scorching your pan, so . . . y'know . . . don't do that.

Extra-virgin olive oil

1 garlic bulb (about 12 cloves), peeled and sliced

Diamond Crystal kosher salt

1 cup raw almonds

¼ cup buckwheat groats

1 tablespoon fresh lemon juice (about ½ lemon)

2 teaspoons grated lemon zest (about 1 lemon)

Flaky salt

1. Set a small pan over medium-high heat and add ½ cup olive oil. Let it heat up (when you add a slice of garlic and it sizzles, it's ready). Add the garlic and swirl to get all the pieces submerged in the oil. Fry until all the garlic slices are golden brown, 3 to 4 minutes. Use a slotted spoon and transfer the garlic to a paper towel to drain. Sprinkle with a pinch of kosher salt.

2. Drain the pan (reserve the oil for any cooking uses you have in the next few days—it's *delicious*) and place the pan back over medium heat. Add the almonds and buckwheat groats and toast, stirring often, until the groats are golden brown, 5 to 6 minutes. Remove the pan from the heat, add the lemon juice, and stir for another 30 seconds.

3. In a medium bowl, combine the garlic chips, toasted almonds, and buckwheat groats, then add the lemon zest and ½ teaspoon flaky salt, stirring to combine. Serve right away or store in a cool, dry place for up to 7 days.

PARMESAN-CRUSTED BUTTER BEANS

Serves 6

Light, cheesy, and crisp, this is the snack I go for when I want something reminiscent of a Cheez-it but more filling and a little more interesting. This is a new take on a popular recipe of mine that uses Parmesan, lemon, and chickpeas, but here I've upgraded them to these butter bean–filled, grown-up cheese crackers (Nabisco, call me). The Parmesan melts around the big, soft beans, forming a contrast of crispy-creamy that's easily sliceable and still has some cracker-y bite. The oven does all the heavy lifting for this recipe—just make sure you're using a rimmed sheet pan because a flat one can lead to a cheese-spilling disaster.

1 (15-ounce) can butter beans, drained and rinsed

6 ounces Parmesan, freshly grated (about 2 cups)

1 tablespoon finely chopped fresh rosemary

1 tablespoon Calabrian chili paste

Extra-virgin olive oil

1. Position a rack in the center of the oven and preheat it to 400°F. Line a quarter-sheet pan with parchment paper.

2. Transfer the butter beans to a cutting board and pat dry.

3. In a small bowl, combine the Parmesan, rosemary, chili paste, and 2 tablespoons oil and mix to combine. Scatter the cheese mixture in a thick, even layer across the lined sheet pan. Layer the butter beans on top, making sure none overlap.

4. Bake until the cheese is golden brown and crisp, 40 to 45 minutes. Remove from the oven and let the beans cool to room temperature.

5. Carefully slide the beans off the parchment paper, slice into big chunks, and serve.

PARMESAN-CRUSTED
BUTTER BEANS

LEMON, ALMOND
& GARLIC CHIPS

SHALLOT
SALMON DIP

GARLIC
EDAMAME DIP

SESAME
NORWEGIAN
CRISPBREADS

SUN-DRIED
TOMATO SPREAD

SESAME NORWEGIAN CRISPBREADS

Makes 9 crispbreads

Norwegian crispbreads, or knekkebrød, aren't technically even close to bread, but what a *treat* they are in and of themselves. They are a nutty, seedy mash-up of ingredients, almost crackerlike in their application, and I find them absolutely delicious. I love them with a thin spread of Tonnato (page 36), as a base for avocado toast, or with smoked salmon and cream cheese. Use them in the same way as you'd eat a slice of toast but just know the crisp factor will be magnified by one thousand.

¾ cup old-fashioned rolled oats

½ cup almond flour

¼ cup flaxseed meal

¼ cup white sesame seeds

¼ cup sunflower seeds

¼ cup pumpkin seeds

½ teaspoon dried rosemary

½ teaspoon dried thyme

½ teaspoon red pepper flakes

Diamond Crystal kosher salt

Extra-virgin olive oil

½ cup warm water

½ tablespoon honey

1. Position a rack in the top of the oven and preheat it to 350°F. Line a quarter sheet pan with parchment paper.

2. In a large bowl, whisk together the oats, almond flour, flaxseed meal, sesame seeds, sunflower seeds, pumpkin seeds, rosemary, thyme, pepper flakes, and ½ teaspoon salt. Drizzle 1 tablespoon olive oil over the mixture and stir to combine.

3. Pour the warm water into a small bowl. Whisk in the honey until it dissolves. Pour this into the oats mixture and stir to combine.

4. Spread this mixture onto the lined sheet pan. Using damp hands or a spatula, flatten it out into a 12 by 9-inch rectangle, about ¼ inch thick. Use a bench scraper to draw small indents on the surface of the rectangle, dividing it into nine even crispbreads 3 by 4 inches in size.

5. Transfer the pan to the oven and bake until deep brown throughout, 35 to 45 minutes.

6. Let the crispbread cool on the pan for 10 to 15 minutes before breaking it into the nine pieces.

A TRIO OF DIPS

I. LOVE. DIPS. And these three are my dream dips, numbered. There's a satisfying salmon dip that doubles as breakfast or a snack, a bright, herbaceous edamame number, and a sun-dried tomato and white bean spread that is so simple it feels like cheating. Together, these three dips complement one another, but they're just as satisfying solo. I typically make one batch at the beginning of the week (either just one or all three) and then scoop them onto Sesame Norwegian Crispbreads (see opposite), whenever I'm feeling slightly snacky. The sun-dried tomato spread on crispbread was in my snack rotation for a few months, until it was quickly replaced by the herby edamame dip with handfuls of raw veggies. So, maybe in spirit, these dips are more competitive than they are complementary—but I promise, I love them all equally.

GARLIC EDAMAME DIP

Makes 1½ cups

While I'm a firm believer that the creamy white bean reigns supreme when it comes to bean-based dips, I like the vibrant color and protein that edamame brings to this version. The flavors here are reminiscent of chimichurri, with a heavy hand on the parsley and garlic right behind it. I serve this a bit underblended to keep some of the texture of the edamame, but if you prefer a smoother spread, give it a few more minutes in the food processor, and it will transform into a texture that's nice and even.

2 cups shelled edamame

2 garlic cloves, peeled but whole

½ cup fresh parsley leaves

2 tablespoons fresh oregano leaves

¼ cup white wine vinegar

¼ teaspoon red pepper flakes

Extra-virgin olive oil

Diamond Crystal kosher salt

In a food processor, combine the edamame, garlic, parsley, oregano, vinegar, and pepper flakes and pulse until most of the ingredients are chopped and begin to combine. Gradually stream in 6 tablespoons olive oil, watching as the edamame purees into a smooth green sauce, adding more oil if needed. Season with ½ teaspoon salt, plus more as needed.

SHALLOT SALMON DIP

Makes 2 cups

My bagel place has a phenomenal baked salmon salad, and it's wild to me that this spread isn't as widely available as its smoked counterpart. Thanks to the delicate, fatty flavor of the salmon, this extra-creamy dip is rich and buttery but not overpoweringly fishy. I've also made this recipe with avocado in place of crème fraîche, which is a great option if you're dairy-free.

8 ounces skin-on salmon (see Note)

Diamond Crystal kosher salt

Freshly ground black pepper

½ cup crème fraîche

1 small shallot, peeled and quartered

2 garlic cloves, peeled but whole

2 tablespoons fresh parsley leaves

2 tablespoons fresh dill, plus sprigs for garnish

2 teaspoons Dijon mustard

½ teaspoon red pepper flakes

1 teaspoon grated lemon zest (about ½ lemon), plus more for garnish

1 . Position a rack in the center of the oven and preheat it to 350°F. Line a sheet pan with parchment paper.

2 . Place the salmon skin-side down on the lined sheet pan and season the fish liberally with salt and black pepper. Bake until completely opaque throughout; check with an instant-read thermometer for an internal temperature of at least 135°F, 14 to 15 minutes.

3 . Meanwhile, in a food processor, combine the crème fraîche, shallot, garlic, parsley, dill, mustard, pepper flakes, lemon zest, ½ teaspoon salt, and a few cracks of black pepper.

4 . When the salmon is out of the oven, let it cool for at least 10 minutes, then flake the salmon away from the skin and add it to the food processor. Pulse until you get a creamy consistency. Season to taste and garnish with a few sprigs of dill and lemon zest.

NOTE: This recipe is great for any leftover baked salmon you might have in the fridge; this cuts the preparation time in half. Since the salmon would already be prepared, use 6 ounces.

SUN-DRIED TOMATO SPREAD

Makes 3 cups

Sun-dried tomatoes often get a bad rap as a "vintage" ingredient, which, frankly, I'm tired of (I mean c'mon, croissants were invented in the 1800s and we *never* gave them this treatment!). Sun-dried tomatoes give a master class in concentrated flavor, making this spread taste as if you had funneled a thousand jammy, sweet, and garlicky confit tomatoes into one white bean dip, while using only five ingredients. It's unfairly easy—plus, after using all the parsley leaves in the other dips, this finds their equally flavorful stems a home.

1 (10-ounce) jar sun-dried tomatoes, packed in olive oil

3 garlic cloves, peeled but whole

1 (15-ounce) can chickpeas or white beans, drained and rinsed

Diamond Crystal kosher salt

½ cup parsley stems, chopped (see Note)

Drain the oil from the sun-dried tomatoes, reserving ¼ cup for the dip. In a food processor, combine the sun-dried tomatoes, garlic, chickpeas, ½ teaspoon salt, the parsley stems, and the reserved sun-dried tomato oil. Process until as smooth as possible, though it will still have some (pleasant!) texture. Season with more salt as needed.

NOTE: You can use parsley leaves instead of stems, I just like using stems in this dip to cut down on food waste, because they taste exactly the same (ditto for cilantro). Store them loosely wrapped in a dry paper towel in an airtight container and they'll stay fresh much longer than their leafy tops.

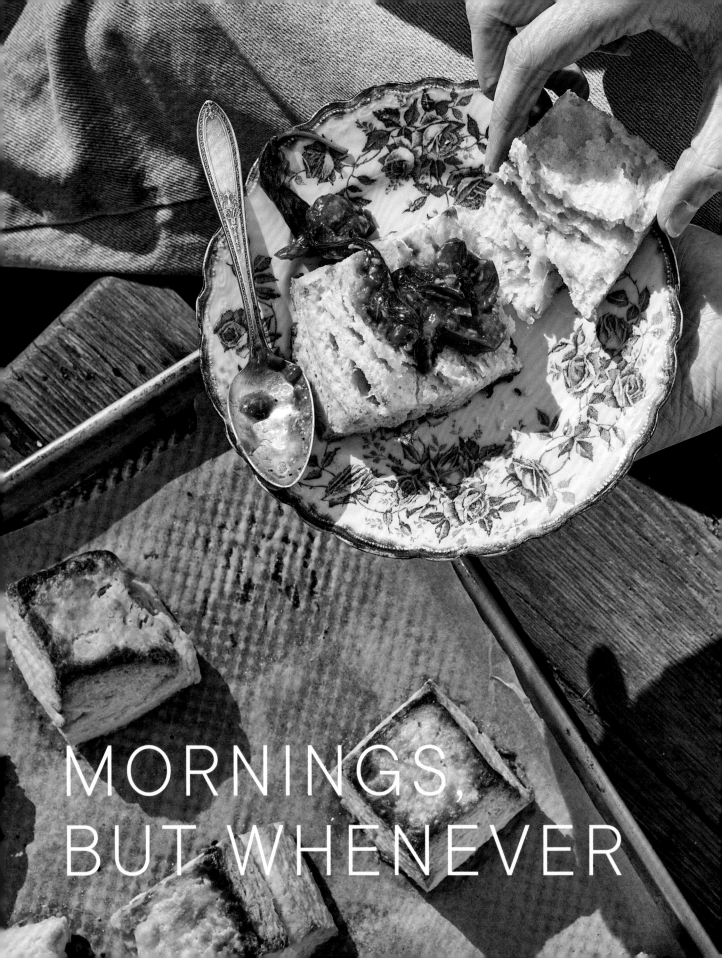

MORNINGS,
BUT WHENEVER

I AM HIGHLY PROTECTIVE OF BREAKFAST, both as a meal and as a way of life. And I know, it is so easy to wake up and make the usual coffee, oatmeal, or two-egg scramble and get on with it. But there's something in me that believes that when breakfast gets a few extra minutes of time and attention, we get those few extra minutes, too—the cooking as your morning reset, so to speak. Plus, when you're done resetting, there are Kimchi-Crusted Poached Eggs (page 78). A win-win.

And while I'm a breakfast romantic, I try not to be unreasonable, because we all do have places to be. There are some very delicious recipes in this chapter that are meant to be your everyday breakfasts, like the Two Famous Oatmeal Bowls (page 73), which are timed and designed to be simple but still give you those extra few minutes in the morning slow down. And the Crispy Sage & Fennel Eggs (page 77), which happen fast but taste nothing like it.

And then there's the second half of this chapter, breakfasts for a crowd, made for when you're cooking a lazy brunch, surrounded by friends who are eager to help out. These recipes remind me that gathering over food is not restricted to dinner. In moments like this, my Miso-Butter Pancakes (page 85) are the MVP of the roster, and Hominy Biscuits & Hot Tomato Spread (page 86) always taste like home.

And while I think nonbreakfast people are crazy (we only get three meals a day, why would you lose one?), I still fit these recipes into their world, too. Most could be a satisfying lunch, a quick dinner (I love the Soft Eggs & Tender Herb Sauce Sandwiches on page 81 for a simple meal) or a late-night sweet snack (think: the Earl Grey Granola with Roasted Pears on page 82). Because if breakfast is all about taking a few extra minutes to slow down, then it makes sense that those moments can happen, well, whenever.

STEWED APPLE
OATMEAL WITH
TORN DATES

ZA'ATAR OATMEAL
WITH A HUNK
OF BUTTER

TWO FAMOUS OATMEAL BOWLS

Please note, these bowls are only called famous because I believe that if I entered them into a competition (in a world where oatmeal competitions exist), they would win. I also think that if I served them at a café, they would become cult classics. So far the term "famous" has been self-given, but I think the blatant confidence is why they taste so good.

ZA'ATAR OATMEAL WITH A HUNK OF BUTTER

Serves 1

There's something delightfully old school about adding a hunk of butter to the middle of a bowl of oats and letting it pool into the center. To date, it's the only way I want my savory oats—salty, rich, and buttery. The one thing that could make it better is a sprinkle of fragrant, earthy za'atar, which gives the bowl a kick of spice and sesame nuttiness that pairs with butter like a best friend. It feels luxurious in its simplicity, and my favorite slow mornings include this bowl and two boiled eggs on the side.

⅔ cup old-fashioned rolled oats

Diamond Crystal kosher salt

2 teaspoons za'atar

1 tablespoon high-quality salted butter, such as Kerrygold

Freshly ground black pepper (optional)

1. Set a medium pot over high heat and add the oats and 1½ cups water. Bring to a boil, then add a pinch of salt and turn the heat down to a simmer. Cook, stirring occasionally, until the oats have thickened, 5 to 7 minutes. Remove the pot from the heat and sprinkle in 1¾ teaspoons of the za'atar and stir to combine. Taste and season with more salt as needed.

2. Pour the oatmeal into a serving bowl and add the butter to the center, letting it melt. Sprinkle the remaining ¼ teaspoon za'atar right on top of the melted butter, add a few big cracks of black pepper, if desired, and eat warm.

STEWED APPLE OATMEAL WITH TORN DATES

Serves 1

The first time I made this oatmeal, I ate it every day for two weeks straight. It's a step away from your normal pour-and-stir oatmeal, with a mix of three ingredients that made me feel as if I had finally broken the café-quality code. First, apples are simmered until they soften, stewing the oats in any sugars they seep out. Second, hand-torn sticky dates are tossed in and melt into the oats, disappearing but leaving a syrupy flavor and molten texture. And third, a smidge of miso, added for a dose of salty, savory contrast that reminds me of Quaker Oats packets, which I love to my core.

1 medium apple of choice, cut into bite-size pieces

⅔ cup old-fashioned rolled oats

½ teaspoon ground cinnamon

2 large Medjool dates, pitted and torn into small pieces

1 teaspoon red miso paste

NOTE: This works amazingly well with pears, peaches, apricots, figs, persimmons, and bananas. With the exception of the pears, all of these fruits can skip the initial boiling step and be added in with the dates and miso.

1. In a medium pot over medium-high heat combine the apple and ¼ cup water. Bring to a simmer, then cover and turn the heat to medium-low. Cook until the apple is fork-tender but not falling apart, 3 to 4 minutes. Add the oats, 1⅓ cups water, and the cinnamon and bring to a soft boil.

2. Add the dates and miso paste and let the mixture thicken, stirring often, for 5 to 7 minutes. The dates will melt into the oats, almost disappearing, and the miso will dissolve. Press the miso into the oats with a spatula if it needs some encouragement.

3. Remove from the heat and let it cool and thicken for an additional 5 to 10 minutes, as desired.

HI, WALTER

CRISPY SAGE & FENNEL EGGS

Serves 1

As a lover of all things Italian sausage, sage and fennel hold a soft spot in my heart. Those flavors give me sausage link nostalgia (without the meat itself), which I copied and pasted straight into fried eggs. This recipe plays with two main textures: the first being the light and crispy fried sage leaves and the second being the crunchy fennel seeds that cook into the egg whites' frizzled edges. An extra-credit texture comes from the over-easy egg yolk, which, when punctured, is best eaten with a thick slice of toast to soak it up.

Extra-virgin olive oil

½ teaspoon fennel seeds

¼ teaspoon red pepper flakes

8 to 10 fresh sage leaves

Diamond Crystal kosher salt

2 large eggs

Freshly ground black pepper

1. Set a small stainless steel pan over medium heat and add 3 tablespoons olive oil. Let the oil heat up until fragrant, 2 to 3 minutes. Add the fennel and pepper flakes and toast, stirring constantly, for 30 seconds as the fennel sizzles. Add the sage leaves and let them fry until crisp, about 1 minute. Season with a pinch of salt.

2. Crack the eggs on top of the fried sage and toasted spices, tilting the pan to the side to baste the whites with any excess spiced oil. The whites should set in less than 2 to 3 minutes, leaving the yolks runny.

3. Remove the eggs from the pan and season with salt and a few cracks of black pepper.

KIMCHI-CRUSTED POACHED EGGS

Serves 1

If you're wondering what the sliced almonds are doing in here, it's an ingredient combination I once had that just stuck with me: The buttery richness and toasty crunch of the almonds against the briny kimchi activate something in my brain that I constantly crave (please try this and agree with me so I don't feel alone). There's something special about popping a poached egg yolk directly into a bowl of those spicy bread crumbs, mixing everything together and eating it with a spoon. You can also do this with jammy eggs as well; just follow the method on page 54.

2 large eggs

1 tablespoon skin-on sliced almonds

¼ cup Sourdough Bread Crumbs (page 46)

½ teaspoon soy sauce

¼ cup kimchi, coarsely chopped

1 teaspoon chili crisp, for serving

A few sprigs of tender fresh herbs, such as dill, mint, cilantro

NOTE: When poaching eggs on a small scale, I've found I don't need any vinegar. Skipping it is just another way to save ingredients on smaller recipes.

1. Set a medium pot over high heat, fill it halfway with water, and bring it to a simmer.

2. Crack one egg at a time into a small-mesh sieve to drain off any excess white. Gently swirl the pot of water to create a whirlpool and carefully drop the egg directly into the center. Allow the egg to cook until the white is fully set, 3 to 5 minutes. Carefully scoop it out and set aside on a paper towel to drain. Repeat with the second egg. (If you're feeling ambitious, you can do both at the same time.)

3. Set a small pan over medium heat and toast the almonds and bread crumbs, until they are golden brown and fragrant, 2 to 3 minutes. Add the soy sauce and kimchi and stir for barely a minute, watching as the soy sauce turns the bread crumbs a deep golden brown.

4. Transfer the kimchi mixture to a serving bowl and top with the eggs. Drizzle with the chili crisp and tear the herbs over everything.

SOFT EGGS & TENDER HERB SAUCE SANDWICHES

Serves 2

These started as Friday-morning breakfast sandwiches that were built of necessity. One Friday morning, I noticed that all the herbs from my last weekend's farmers' market trip were on their last legs, and so by blanching, I saved them for one last use. But after enough rounds of this tangy, green tender-herb-egg-salad-of-sorts impressing the hell out of me (and others!), I formally moved it from "necessity" recipe to "favorites." A high honor.

Diamond Crystal kosher salt

2 cups tender fresh herbs, such as parsley, basil, dill, cilantro

4 large eggs

2 garlic cloves, grated

½ teaspoon red pepper flakes

½ teaspoon Aleppo pepper flakes

1 teaspoon grated lemon zest (about ½ lemon)

3 tablespoons fresh lemon juice (about 1 lemon)

Extra-virgin olive oil

Freshly ground black pepper

2 English muffins, split and toasted

1. Set a large pot over high heat, bring 2 quarts water to a boil, and season with 1 teaspoon salt. Add the herbs and boil for less than a minute. Scoop them out with a mesh sieve and run them under cool tap water, until they are cool enough to handle. Squeeze out any excess moisture with your hands and coarsely chop them.

2. Add the eggs to the pot and boil for 7 minutes.

3. Meanwhile, in a medium bowl, combine the chopped herbs, garlic, red pepper flakes, Aleppo pepper flakes, lemon zest and juice, and 3 tablespoons olive oil. Mix and season with salt and black pepper to taste.

4. Scoop the eggs out of the pot and run them under cool tap water for a few seconds to cool. Peel and quarter the eggs, adding them to the bowl with the herbs. Mix to combine and season with more salt and black pepper as needed.

5. Pile the herbed egg mixture onto the English muffins. Wrap in aluminum foil for a great to-go sandwich or eat immediately.

EARL GREY GRANOLA WITH ROASTED PEARS

Makes 5 cups of granola

This Earl Grey–infused recipe came about after a summer of coffee shop granola impulse buys and a few too many iced London Fog lattes. (That was before I swapped tea for my beloved Americanos, but I used to be a dedicated Earl Grey girl.) And in true London Fog fashion, this granola is lightly spiced, not too sweet, and injects a feeling of coziness in every bite. Since we're already turning on the oven, I pair this with sink-your-spoon-in pears that roast at the same time as the granola. The recipe makes 5 cups, which is enough to use a little over half for serving and the rest for later. So, yes, the pears are optional, but if you're making the granola already, you might as well make a roasty, buttery partner for it.

8 tablespoons salted butter

2 Earl Grey teabags

3 medium Bosc pears, halved and cored

2 cups old-fashioned rolled oats

¼ cup flaxseed meal

¼ cup pumpkin seeds

2 tablespoons hemp hearts

½ teaspoon ground cinnamon

Diamond Crystal kosher salt

2 teaspoons vanilla extract

⅓ cup honey

1 large egg white

Milk of choice, for serving

1. Equally stagger two racks in the oven and preheat it to 325°F.

2. Set a small pan over medium heat and add the butter. Let the butter fully melt, then tear open the tea bags, pour in the tea leaves, and swirl to combine. The mixture will begin to bubble slightly, so turn the heat to low and stir for 2 to 3 minutes. Remove the pan from the heat.

3. Place two pear halves a piece on a sheet of aluminum foil, cut side up. Spoon 1 tablespoon of the Earl Grey butter mixture over the cut sides, and wrap them into a packet with the fold on top, being careful there are no cuts or punctures in the foil. Set them on the bottom rack of the oven to bake for 30 minutes.

4. In a large bowl, combine the oats, flaxseed meal, pumpkin seeds, hemp hearts, cinnamon, and ½ teaspoon salt. Pour the remaining 5 tablespoons butter mixture into the bowl, add the vanilla and honey, and mix well.

5. In a small bowl, whisk the egg white until foamy. Add that to the bowl with the granola mix and stir to coat everything evenly.

6. Line a sheet pan with parchment paper and spread the granola on the sheet. Transfer to the top rack of the oven to bake until golden brown and dry to the touch, 25 to 30 minutes.

7. To serve, add half a pear to each bowl and top with a heaping scoop of granola and a splash of milk. Drizzle on any remaining buttery pear juice left over in the foil; it will dot on top of the milk, which is supremely satisfying.

8. This recipe will leave you with some leftover granola, which you can store in a cool, dry place for up to 1 week.

MISO-BUTTER PANCAKES

Makes 15 to 20 large pancakes

If I had a trade secret recipe, this should have been it. Good thing I don't believe in secrets, which is why this recipe has been shared between family and friends, just waiting for its formal debut. These buttery, golden pancakes have a subtle umami note from miso that makes them salty and sweet at the same time. The batter is on the thinner side, meant to griddle into lacy edges and a fluffy interior, with just a few oats added for a hint of chew. The recipe is designed to balance perfectly with maple syrup, because any pancake feels a little naked without it.

8 tablespoons / 113g salted butter, plus more for griddling and serving

2 tablespoons white miso paste

1½ cups / 210g all-purpose flour

⅔ cup / 65g old-fashioned rolled oats

3 tablespoons dark brown sugar

Diamond Crystal kosher salt

1½ teaspoons baking powder

1¾ cups / 420ml whole milk, though any milk will work

2 large eggs

Maple syrup, for serving

1. Set a small pan over medium heat and add the butter. Let the butter fully melt, then whisk in the miso. Continue to cook for 2 to 3 minutes, stirring occasionally, since the butter will begin to foam. The milk solids will separate from the butter and form flecks at the bottom of the pan. Continue to stir until the flecks are golden brown. The miso will also toast with the butter. There will be some larger pieces, but that's okay! Keep mixing until the butter mixture is extremely toasted into an almost burnt, dark brown. Remove from the heat and set aside.

2. In a large bowl, whisk together the flour, oats, brown sugar, 1 teaspoon salt, and baking powder.

3. In a small bowl, whisk together the milk and miso-brown butter. Add the eggs and whisk until smooth. Pour this mixture into the dry ingredients and mix until you have a smooth batter. This batter will thicken as you preheat the pan.

4. Set a large pan over medium heat and wait until you can add a few drops of water and they form balls that bounce around the pan; this makes it so your pan will not need greasing. Turn the heat to medium-low. Working in batches, use a ¼-cup scoop to pour the batter into large, even pancakes, each 4 to 5 inches in diameter. Cook until golden, 2 to 3 minutes on each side.

5. Serve with maple syrup drizzled on top.

HOMINY BISCUITS & HOT TOMATO SPREAD

Makes 8 biscuits

These cornmeal biscuits are meant to be wholesome and buttery, with distinct, almost countable layers. White cornmeal, more specifically masa, a finely ground hominy, has a more delicate, tender texture than yellow cornmeal. I buy P.A.N. white cornmeal, which is not only crazy affordable but the only cornmeal I recommend for fluffy arepas at home (after you finish making these biscuits, of course). The hot tomato spread is a bonus, because even if you're not making biscuits, you can steal that recipe to go with cheese plates, sandwiches, or the crispbreads on page 66.

HOMINY BISCUITS

16 tablespoons / 226g salted butter, chilled

2 cups / 280g all-purpose flour, plus more for dusting

1 cup / 140g white corn masa harina or white cornmeal, plus more for dusting

¼ cup / 50g sugar

1 tablespoon baking powder

Diamond Crystal kosher salt

1⅓ cups / 300ml cold buttermilk, plus more for brushing

HOT TOMATO SPREAD

Extra-virgin olive oil

1 pound (1 pint) cherry tomatoes, halved

1 Fresno pepper, seeded and finely chopped

¼ cup fresh basil leaves

2 garlic cloves, grated

Diamond Crystal kosher salt

Freshly ground black pepper

1 tablespoon red wine vinegar

2 teaspoons dark brown sugar

1. Make the hominy biscuits: Either grate the butter with a cheese grater or cut it into small cubes; chill in the freezer while you prep the other ingredients.

2. Line a sheet pan with parchment paper.

3. In a large bowl, whisk together the flours, sugar, baking powder, and 2 teaspoons salt. Add the butter into the flour, tossing to coat each butter piece in flour, and flattening any big butter chunks as you go. When the butter is incorporated, slowly pour the buttermilk around the edge of the dough, and use a fork to combine into a crumbly dough. Transfer the dough onto a clean (preferably cold) work surface. Using your hands, press the dough together. Fold it in half, then press down. Dust the top with cornmeal, rotate 90 degrees and repeat the fold again. You'll begin to see the dough start to come together. Rotate and repeat one more time.

4. From there, pat the dough into a rough rectangle that is 1½ inches high.

5. Cut the dough into nine square biscuits. Transfer them to the lined pan and chill in the fridge while the oven preheats.

6. Position a rack in the center of the oven and preheat it to 375°F.

7. Before baking, brush each biscuit with a layer of buttermilk. Bake until golden, 25 to 30 minutes.

8. Meanwhile, make the tomato spread: Set a small pan over medium heat and add 2 tablespoons olive oil. Let the oil heat up for 2 to 3 minutes, then add the cherry tomatoes and Fresno peppers. Cook, stirring occasionally, for 3 to 4 minutes to allow the tomatoes to break down.

9 . Add the basil and garlic and cook, stirring often, until the tomatoes burst and are jammy, an additional 6 to 9 minutes. Season with a pinch of salt and a few cracks of black pepper. When the tomatoes are fully collapsed, turn off the heat. Deglaze the pan with the vinegar and stir in the brown sugar. Set aside. The mixture will thicken into a chunky, almost spreadable jam.

10 . When the biscuits are out of the oven, serve alongside the tomato spread.

PUT IT ON BREAD

IF WE WERE TALKING ABOUT A LAST-MEAL SITUATION,
mine would need to include some kind (or multiple kinds) of
bread. Even on a less serious, day-to-day scale, I find myself
reaching for bread more often than not. My after-school snack
from ages five to seven was a single piece of white bread,
smashed down and rolled up, eaten right before ballet class. A
nutritional powerhouse—but also proof that I was born, raised,
and bred on bread.

Today, it's fair to say bread is my favorite base. If it isn't
already bread, I want to find a way to put it on bread. If I'm
feeling lazy, I turn to a toast, and if a dish feels a little lonely, it's
nothing a pairing with sourdough can't fix. Anything that needs
a little bolstering, I can usually fix with bread as the base—
because nothing says breakfast, lunch, or dinner like a tall, piled
fork-and-knife toast.

The recipes that follow range from light to substantial, from
a light and sweet persimmon toast (see page 90) to a more
filling Ricotta Bowl with Poblano-Herb Sauce (page 105), which,
yes, is a bowl . . . on toast.

While none of these recipes technically needs bread (well,
except for The Perfect Heirloom Tomato Toast on page 101,
which would feel a little floppy without it), each recipe was
specifically chosen because bread enhances it tenfold. If it's not
a texture play, I'm using the bread to soak up flavors that might
otherwise be lost off the tip of a fork or forgotten at the bottom
of a bowl. I'm still going to encourage you to add bread to other
recipes in this book, but in this chapter specifically, bread is
nonnegotiable.

JAMMY PERSIMMON WITH HONEY & LIME

Serves 2

I learned the technique of this recipe through the grapevine of persimmon lovers at the a farmers' market. Freeze it overnight, let it thaw on your kitchen counter the next morning, and it turns into "nature's jam." Persimmon, in all its juicy, mystical glory, is one of the most fascinating fruits. Like tomatoes, there are only a few months a year when they're fantastic (pssst . . . it's October through December in the Northeast). Softly sweet, they have a light flavor akin to baking spices and a texture that I can only describe as *glossy*. This will work with both main varietals of persimmons, though I do recommend the tall and jiggly Hachiya if you can find them.

1 persimmon (preferably Hachiya, but Fuyu will work as well)

1 tablespoon fresh lime juice (about ½ lime)

¼ teaspoon ground cardamom

2 tablespoons roasted, salted pistachios, shelled and chopped

½ teaspoon grated lime zest, (about ½ lime)

4 or 5 fresh mint leaves

Labneh, enough for a smooth smear

2 thick slices sourdough bread, toasted

2 teaspoons honey

1. Thoroughly wash and dry the persimmon and place it in the freezer overnight, either on a plate or in a container.

2. When ready to use, cut off the top of the persimmon and cut the fruit into cubes while it is still firm. You can peel it if you like; that's personal preference. Add the pieces to a small bowl with the lime juice, cover with a plate or dish towel, and let it thaw on the counter. This will take about 1 hour, but see the Note below for how to speed up the process.

3. Once the persimmon has thawed, sprinkle in the cardamom and gently mash with a fork, easing the persimmon down into big, jammy, spreadable pieces.

4. Add the pistachios to a small bowl, add the lime zest, tear in the mint, and toss.

5. Spread a thin layer of labneh on the toast. Spoon the persimmon mixture on top, drizzle with the honey, and generously garnish with the pistachio and mint.

NOTE: To speed up the thawing process, fill a bowl with boiling water, then empty the bowl and add the persimmon. Cover the bowl and wait for 10 minutes for the persimmon to thaw.

TURMERIC-SIZZLED TOAST WITH SUNGOLD TOMATOES

Serves 2

On the flavor-to-simplicity scale, this recipe is off the charts. The coconut milk mingles with the sweet tomato juices that pool in the pan, creating (in my humble opinion) the only other "liquid gold" that exists outside of starchy pasta water. Piling this creamy, spiced tomato mixture on top of toast gives you the coveted sensation of "crispy-gone-soggy" that is one of life's most delicious situations.

Extra-virgin olive oil

1 teaspoon ground turmeric

Diamond Crystal kosher salt

2 thick slices bread, any kind

1 pound (1 pint) Sungold tomatoes, halved

2 garlic cloves, grated

2 teaspoons grated fresh ginger

¼ teaspoon ground coriander

¼ teaspoon ground cumin

¼ teaspoon smoked paprika

¼ teaspoon Aleppo pepper flakes, plus more for sprinkling

2 tablespoons canned unsweetened full-fat coconut milk

4 or 5 fresh basil leaves, for garnish

4 or 5 fresh mint leaves, for garnish

Freshly ground black pepper

1. Set a pan over medium heat and pour in 1 tablespoon olive oil. Add ½ teaspoon of the turmeric and a pinch of salt and swirl to make the oil evenly golden. Once the oil is fragrant, add one slice of bread to the pan and toast until crisp and bright golden yellow, about 2 minutes on each side. Repeat the steps for the second slice of bread. Keep any remaining turmeric oil in the pan.

2. To the turmeric oil in the pan, add a drizzle of olive oil and the tomatoes. Cook for 1 to 2 minutes, stirring occasionally as the tomatoes collapse. Add the garlic, ginger, coriander, cumin, paprika, and pepper flakes. Season with salt. Cook for an additional 3 to 4 minutes, stirring occasionally as the tomatoes release their juices and come to a soft simmer. Add the coconut milk and cook for another 1 to 2 minutes, letting the mixture reduce slightly, allowing the flavors to meld. Remove from the heat and season with salt and black pepper.

3. Scoop half the tomatoes onto each slice of toast, making sure to gather pan juices with every spoonful. Tear up the basil and mint and scatter on top. Top with a few cracks of black pepper and a sprinkle of pepper flakes.

DRIPPY HARISSA EGGPLANT WITH SPOON-OVER SAUCE

Serves 4

The description of eggplant as "seedy" and "creamy" always turned me off. If you replace those adjectives with "rich," "meaty," and "hearty," its potential completely transforms. While roasting the eggplant takes some time, we're letting it melt into its natural texture, which will then suck up this umami-rich harissa broth like a sponge. Make sure to scoop up little spoonfuls of sweet-and-spicy harissa caramelizing around the edges of your pan to get the most out of all that concentrated flavor—that's where the spoon-over comes in.

1 large eggplant (1¾ pounds)

⅓ cup spicy harissa paste (I love Mina or New York Shuk)

2 tablespoons soy sauce

1 tablespoon Worcestershire sauce

1 tablespoon light brown sugar

Extra-virgin olive oil

4 thick slices sourdough bread

⅔ cup Sourdough Bread Crumbs (page 46)

Diamond Crystal kosher salt

¼ cup fresh dill, finely chopped

¼ cup fresh chives, finely chopped

1 lemon, for squeezing (optional)

NOTE: You can also add the dill, chives, and lemon to the pan and serve this dip-style as a fun date-night trick.

1. Position a rack in the center of the oven and preheat it to 425°F. Line a sheet pan with parchment paper.

2. Halve the eggplant lengthwise. Score the flesh of the eggplant diagonally, then place the halves flesh-side down on the lined sheet pan. Roast the eggplant until the skin is charred and it looks a bit collapsed, 40 to 45 minutes.

3. While the eggplant is roasting, in a small bowl, whisk together the harissa, soy sauce, Worcestershire sauce, brown sugar, and ⅓ cup water. Set aside.

4. Set a deep sauté pan over medium heat and add 1 tablespoon olive oil. Pan-fry the bread slices, toasting until golden, 2 to 3 minutes on each side. Remove the bread and add the bread crumbs to the pan, toasting them for 3 to 4 minutes, stirring occasionally so as not to burn. Season with salt and transfer the bread crumbs to a small bowl and carefully wipe out the pan.

5. When the eggplant is finished roasting, scrape the flesh out of the skin into a bowl (discard the skin and stem). Place the sauté pan back over medium heat and add 1 tablespoon olive oil. Add the eggplant flesh and the harissa mixture and mix everything together with a spatula to coat. Bring the sauce to a simmer and simmer for 5 to 6 minutes to thicken slightly. Remove the pan from the heat. Scatter the bread crumbs evenly over the eggplant but don't mix them in.

6. To serve, scoop a generous helping of crumb-topped eggplant onto each slice of bread and spoon over any remaining sauce in the pan. Sprinkle with the chopped dill, chives, and a squeeze of lemon juice (if using) and serve.

BROCCOLINI, BALSAMIC, BURRATA, AMEN

Serves 2

Like most cheese, all burrata had to do was exist for me to love it. On this melty toast, the burrata comes in at the end, but it's most definitely the star. Thin strands of broccolini get all crispy in the oven, balsamic caramelizes on the edges, and a swipe of roasted red pepper paste sets up the toast for everything to pile on top. Plus, you can make the red pepper spread ahead of time to use throughout the week on sandwiches, grain bowls, pasta, and/or multiple versions of this toast (*I vote for multiple versions of this toast*).

½ cup jarred roasted red peppers, packed in oil, drained

Diamond Crystal kosher salt

Freshly ground black pepper

8 ounces broccolini, bottom 2 inches of stalks removed

Extra-virgin olive oil

¼ teaspoon red pepper flakes

2 teaspoons balsamic vinegar

2 servings ciabatta bread, split open horizontally

4 ounces burrata cheese

1. Equally stagger two racks in the oven and preheat it to 425°F. Line two sheet pans with parchment paper.

2. In a blender, combine the roasted red peppers, 1 tablespoon water, a pinch of kosher salt, and a few cracks of black pepper and blend until fully smooth. Set the roasted pepper paste aside.

3. Slice the broccolini down the center, creating long, thin strips. I keep them in long strips for the look, but you could also cut them into bite-size pieces. Spread them out on one of the lined pans and toss with 1 tablespoon olive oil. Season with the pepper flakes and salt and black pepper to taste and mix.

4. Roast the broccolini on the top rack of the oven until it is bright and green, 8 to 10 minutes. Remove the broccolini from the oven, drizzle with the balsamic vinegar, and mix with tongs to coat.

5. Set the ciabatta cut-side up on the second pan. Add the ciabatta to the top rack and move the broccolini to the lower rack. Bake both until the broccolini is crisped and slightly charred and the ciabatta is toasted, 8 to 9 minutes.

6. Remove the broccolini and ciabatta from the oven. Tear the burrata into 2-inch pieces directly over the broccolini and mix together on the pan so the heat from the pan kind of melts the burrata into the broccolini.

7. Add a swipe of the roasted pepper paste to the bottom of each slice of ciabatta and pile the broccolini mix on top. Dot with more pepper paste if you like, season with a few cracks of black pepper, and eat immediately.

SALAD TOAST WITH SUMAC RADICCHIO

Serves 2

Meet salad toast, where essentially the bread is one big crouton and the salad sits on top of it, prepped for fork-and-knife eating. Radicchio is one of my favorite chicories for said "salad toasting," and here it's tossed in a sweet, acidic dressing and a generous hit of sumac, which adds a citrusy, floral note and balances any bitterness. The giant crouton is toasted in za'atar-infused oil to make sure it doesn't feel forgotten in the flavor department. And think of the salty feta-plus-yogurt mix as a suggestion, since a spread of ricotta or cashew cream would be equally as good.

1 tablespoon honey

½ teaspoon sumac

2 tablespoons white wine vinegar

Extra-virgin olive oil

Diamond Crystal kosher salt

1 small head radicchio (¾ pound), finely chopped

1 Persian (mini) cucumber, sliced paper thin

15 fresh mint leaves, torn

¼ cup whole-milk yogurt

2 ounces feta cheese, stored in brine (reserve the brine)

2 teaspoons za'atar

2 thick slices sourdough bread

3 roasted, salted pistachios, for serving (optional)

1. In a large bowl, whisk together the honey, sumac, vinegar, 1 tablespoon olive oil, and ¼ teaspoon salt. Add the radicchio, cucumber, and mint and toss to coat.

2. Spoon the yogurt into a small bowl. Crumble in the feta and mix into a spread. Thin it with 1 tablespoon of the salty feta brine.

3. Set a large pan over medium heat and add 1 tablespoon olive oil and 1 teaspoon of the za'atar, swirling the za'atar into the oil. Add one slice of sourdough on top and toast for 2 minutes on each side. Repeat with the second slice of bread, more oil, and the remaining za'atar.

4. Top each toast with a spread of the feta mixture and a healthy serving of the radicchio. If desired, grate the pistachios over everything or coarsely chop and sprinkle them on top. Eat with a fork and knife.

THE PERFECT HEIRLOOM TOMATO TOAST

Serves 2

While the standard opinion is the classic tomato plus mayo plus toast combo is not to be touched, I like to mix up a few ingredients that make a tomato toast, to me, feel perfect. And if you're reading this book, odds are you and I probably have similar tastes. So in a world where there might be a toast you're used to seeing, this combination has a little funk, fragrance, and nuttiness from caraway seeds, a bit of hot sauce heat, and a whole lot of salty butter that picks up touches of tomato juice and seeps into the crevices of the sourdough. It's a tomato dream. And my kind of perfect.

1 large heirloom tomato

1 teaspoon caraway seeds

4 tablespoons salted butter, at room temperature

4 thick slices sourdough bread, toasted

2 teaspoons hot sauce, such as Frank's RedHot

Flaky salt

Freshly ground black pepper

1. Starting from the bottom, slice the tomato crosswise into thin slices.

2. Set a small stainless steel pan over medium heat and toast the caraway seeds until fragrant, 2 to 3 minutes.

3. Evenly spread the butter onto each slice of bread. Add ½ teaspoon of the hot sauce to each. Lay 1 or 2 tomato slices on top, enough to cover the bread. Scatter the caraway seeds on top and sprinkle with a large pinch of flaky salt and a few cracks of black pepper. Eat immediately.

CRUST-OFF AVOCADO TOAST

Serves 4

Mixing cheese with avocado felt criminal, until I realized that putting bread crumbs on top of bread felt equally illegal. It's an avocado toast rebellion, and I'm here for it. You'll use the crust of fluffy brioche (or whatever sandwich bread you prefer) to make bread crumbs that get baked with salty green olives, a few favorite spices, and a pile of Parmesan for a zesty, crunchy topping. This is my fiancé's favorite recipe of the book, saying it's because he "gets the texture of the crust, without it being in the way of my bites," and also "it's like a pizza place met avocado toast!" I'm not sure which is more compelling, but I'll let you decide.

4 square slices brioche or any bread you prefer, crusts removed and reserved

⅓ cup pitted green olives, such as Castelvetrano, finely chopped

½ teaspoon fennel seeds

½ teaspoon red pepper flakes

2 garlic cloves, grated

½ ounce Parmesan cheese, freshly grated (about 3 tablespoons)

1 teaspoon grated lemon zest (about ½ lemon)

Extra-virgin olive oil

1 medium avocado

1 tablespoon fresh lemon juice (about ½ lemon)

Diamond Crystal kosher salt

Freshly ground black pepper

1. Equally stagger two racks in the oven and preheat it to 350°F.

2. In a food processor, pulse the reserved brioche crusts until fine bread crumbs form. In a medium bowl, combine the crust crumbs, olives, fennel seeds, pepper flakes, garlic, Parmesan, lemon zest, and 1 tablespoon olive oil. Mix well.

3. Move the bread crumb mixture to a sheet pan and the four slices of bread to another. Place the bread crumbs on the lower rack and the slices of bread on the top rack. Toast until golden, 12 to 15 minutes, stirring the bread crumbs halfway through.

4. While the bread crumbs and toast are in the oven, mash up the avocado in a small bowl and add the lemon juice. Season with salt and a few cracks of black pepper.

5. Spread the avocado evenly on each slice of bread and sprinkle with a generous amount of the bread crumb mixture. Drizzle with more olive oil and lemon juice, as desired.

NOTE: Depending on your verve for bread crumbs, this recipe might make a bit more than you need. Keep it for pastas, vegetables, fish, or salads. Store in the pantry or fridge for up to 5 days.

RICOTTA BOWLS WITH POBLANO-HERB SAUCE

Serves 2

These bowls are making their debut here because they truly cannot be served without bread. I'm firmly in a camp that believes ricotta is a protein, and a protein makes a meal, so bowls of cheese and vegetables drizzled in olive oil and scooped up with bread? A meal. Full stop. Here, the poblano and tomatoes are roasted together on a sheet pan, but the poblano is then scooped away to transform into a cutting board herb sauce that can only be described as ricotta's best friend. I love a fluffy Sweet Potato Focaccia (page 246) with this, but you can also use whatever you have on hand, because this is a recipe that was born to be with bread—literally any bread will do.

1 large poblano pepper, seeded and halved

1 pound (1 pint) cherry tomatoes or tomatoes on the vine, halved

5 garlic cloves, peeled but whole

Extra-virgin olive oil

2 tablespoons roasted, salted pistachios

1 cup fresh cilantro leaves

½ cup fresh basil leaves

2 tablespoons red wine vinegar

½ teaspoon ground cumin

Diamond Crystal kosher salt

1 cup whole-milk ricotta

2 rectangles Sweet Potato Focaccia (page 246) or two servings of your favorite focaccia

Freshly ground black pepper

Lemon wedges, for serving

1 . Position a rack in the top third of the oven and preheat it to 425°F.

2 . Place the poblano skin-side up, tomatoes, and garlic cloves on a sheet pan. Drizzle with some olive oil and roast until the pepper and tomatoes have softened and the garlic is light golden, 10 to 15 minutes. Switch the oven to broil for another 3 to 5 minutes. The tomatoes should be charred and bursting, the poblano should be blackened, and the garlic should be deeply golden. Broilers are finicky, so keep an eye on yours and remove them when you see significant char marks.

3 . Transfer the poblano to a small bowl, cover with a lid or plate, and let it steam for 10 minutes. Gently peel off the skin.

4 . On a large cutting board, finely chop the pistachios, cilantro, and basil and set to the side of the board. Place the poblano and 2 of the roasted garlic cloves on the cutting board. Finely chop, until no piece is bigger than a lentil. Combine with the herbs and nuts and give a few more chops to bring the cutting board sauce together.

5 . Transfer it all to a bowl and add the vinegar, cumin, and salt to taste. Add the charred tomatoes and remaining 3 garlic cloves and give a quick toss to coat in the poblano-herb sauce.

6 . To serve, start with a large scoop of ricotta in each of the two bowls, pile the tomato-poblano sauce in the center, and add a thick slice of focaccia on the side. Add a few cracks of black pepper and drizzle with a little olive oil and a squeeze of lemon.

BUTTERNUT SQUASH GRILLED CHEESE WITH PICKLED FENNEL

Serves 6

This recipe is grilled cheese for a crowd, inspired by Nancy Silverton's grilled cheese night at the iconic LA restaurant République, where she stood in a center kitchen making thick and melty grilled cheeses to order. I've desperately wanted to re-create the same feeling at home, with friends instead of paying customers and with a few more vegetables in the mix to make the meal feel substantial and satisfying. The butternut and cheese filling is modeled after pommes aligot (a French potato dish that is more dairy than potatoes). Make that first, then scoop, spread, and sear the grilled cheeses to order. It's a big recipe, so both the filling and the slaw can be made beforehand. Store in the fridge for up to 2 days.

1 small fennel bulb, stalks and fronds removed, thinly sliced

⅓ cup fresh dill, stems removed

¼ cup white wine vinegar

Diamond Crystal kosher salt

Freshly ground black pepper

1 small butternut squash (1½ pounds), halved and seeded

3 tablespoons salted butter, plus more for grilling the sandwiches

2 garlic cloves, finely grated

1 tablespoon finely chopped fresh rosemary

1 tablespoon fresh thyme leaves

5 fresh sage leaves, finely chopped

1 teaspoon smoked paprika

½ teaspoon ground nutmeg

½ teaspoon cayenne pepper

4 ounces Gouda cheese, freshly grated (about 1½ packed cups)

1. Position a rack in the center of the oven and preheat it to 400°F. Line a sheet pan with parchment paper.

2. In a large bowl, combine the fennel, dill, vinegar, a generous pinch of kosher salt, and a few cracks of pepper. Toss to quickly "pickle" and set aside.

3. Set the squash cut-side down on the lined sheet pan and roast until it is fork-tender, 30 to 40 minutes.

4. When the squash is cool enough to handle, peel off the skin and use a potato masher, a fork, or a spoon (and a dream) and smash the squash until it resembles mashed potatoes. It won't be completely smooth but do your best and don't discard any excess liquid.

5. Set a large Dutch oven over medium heat and melt 1 tablespoon of the butter. Add the garlic, rosemary, thyme, and sage and stir until they become fragrant, 30 to 45 seconds. Add the butternut squash, season with the paprika, nutmeg, cayenne, and a pinch of salt and stir. Add all the grated cheeses to a bowl and mix. Add about one-third of the combined cheeses, 1 tablespoon of the butter, and the cream. Turn the heat to medium-low and cook, stirring constantly, until you see the butter and cheeses melt together and begin to form a stringy butternut mash. Add another one-third of the cheese and stir until fully melted, then add the remaining cheese and stir until it melts in. Season to taste with additional salt and black pepper and remove the Dutch oven from the heat. The butternut squash should be one homogenous, cheesy mess.

4 ounces Cheddar cheese, freshly grated (about 1½ packed cups)

1 tablespoon heavy cream

12 slices rye bread or any bread you prefer

6 . Butter one side of each bread slice. Set a large pan over medium heat and add the remaining 1 tablespoon butter to the pan. Let it melt, then place the bread buttered-side down. Add ⅓ cup (or more if you like) of the butternut squash mash to the unbuttered side of the bread and spread it evenly. Place another slice of bread on top, buttered-side up and pan-grill until toasted and golden brown on both sides, 3 to 4 minutes per side. Repeat the steps for the remaining slices of bread.

7 . Before serving, peel back the top slice of bread and add a few slices of the fennel slaw. Halve the sandwich right before eating and savor the cheese pull.

SALADS,
THE GOOD KIND

I LIKE HOW IN THE PAST DECADE OR SO, salads have gone from an afterthought to very much the stars of the show. And I promise, if you think eating salads gets old, you're eating the wrong salads. I can only say this so firmly because I, too, was once caught in the wrong salad arena. But salads are a game to play. There's a certain way to build a plate of vegetables to peak craveability, and that's why I think crafting the perfect salad is so fun.

Salads are all about variation, texture play, the size and cut of each ingredient, mixing warm and cool, grating things over, matching crispy vegetables with crunchy toppings, and making sure that if there is a dressing, it's perfectly paired, and if there isn't, then lemon juice or a hint of vinegar will be just enough to bring the plate to life. I learned it was about finding the good olive oil (or the good *enough* olive oil) and making sure to season your salads the same way you'd season your steak.

Each of the salads in this chapter reflects different sides of my salad-building style. Some are full-meal worthy, like the Baked Kale Salad with Chili Quinoa (page 113), while others are giving the side salad a rebrand (see A Garden Salad to Make You Love Garden Salad, page 110). Some are heavier and filling (see A Spoon Salad, page 122), while others are light with an emphasis on crisp (see Celery Salad with Hunks of Parmesan, page 117). But all of them had to pass the test: Would I make it again and again? If the answer was yes, they earned their place in this chapter—as a salad, but one of the good kinds.

A GARDEN SALAD TO MAKE YOU LOVE GARDEN SALAD

Serves 4 as a side

There is a Little Gem lettuce from a farm in Lancaster County in Pennsylvania that I have lovingly dubbed "the good lettuce." It's super light and almost buttery in texture. Normally, I'm not drawn to lettuce-based-salads (so-called garden salads have hurt me one too many times), but if Little Gems are involved, I'm in. And the general public seems to agree; every time I serve this at a dinner, it always disappears at a speed that you do not expect, with questions of *how is this so good?* I credit the rave reviews (Rotten Tomatoes Certified Fresh!) to a sneaky balance of salt, sweet, and more herbs than you'd think. The other secret: grated walnuts, which add the subtlest texture that people don't notice until they fall in love.

1 head Little Gem or red leaf lettuce

2 cups tender fresh herbs, think parsley, cilantro, dill, and mint

2 garlic cloves, grated

1 teaspoon grated lemon zest (about ½ lemon)

3 tablespoons fresh lemon juice (about 1 lemon)

2 teaspoons honey

Extra-virgin olive oil

Freshly ground black pepper

Flaky salt

2 or 3 walnuts, toasted, for grating (optional)

1. Wash and dry the lettuce and herbs very well. This helps the lemon juice and olive oil cling to the leaves. Roughly tear the lettuce and herbs together and set aside.

2. In a large bowl, whisk together the garlic, lemon zest and juice, honey, and 2 tablespoons olive oil. Add the lettuce and herbs and toss with clean hands. Season with lots of cracks of black pepper and a hefty pinch of salt. Give another mix, taste, and season with more salt and pepper, as needed.

3. Use a rasp-style grater to grate the toasted walnuts over the salad for some extra texture if you'd like, but otherwise, place the bowl on the table to eat with whatever else you're preparing.

A NOTE ON DRYING LETTUCE

Drying your lettuce is one of the more valuable life skills my salad spinner taught me. When lettuce is still a bit wet, from your salad spinner or otherwise, it is nearly impossible for any dressing or oil to cling to the greens. Try salad spinning in much smaller batches, which takes 30 more seconds but is worth every single one. If you are salad-spinner-less, wrap your cleaned lettuce head in a kitchen towel and give it a few good shakes over the sink, and when in doubt, there's always the option of separating the leaves and dabbing with a kitchen towel.

BAKED KALE SALAD WITH CHILI QUINOA

Serves 4

Anytime the weather dips below 50°F, it is unofficially baked salad season—the season when all my salads turn roasted and hearty. And I don't care if my love of kale is very circa 2012, *I love kale*. It has heft, it has crunch, and it holds up to any heat or toppings I throw at it. This roasted kale and cabbage salad stretches between side salad and full meal, with a chili-crispy quinoa topping that adds a touch more protein. The dressing is a take on agrodolce, which is a sweet-sour Italian condiment that thrives on sturdy vegetables, so feel free to bookmark it for any other salads you plan on making throughout our coveted baked salad season.

¾ cup quinoa, any type

1 bunch Lacinato kale
(16 ounces), thinly sliced

1 head savoy cabbage
(24 ounces), thinly sliced

2 tablespoons avocado oil

Diamond Crystal kosher salt

Freshly ground black pepper

2 tablespoons chili oil of choice
(I prefer Calabrian chili oil or
Brightland Ardor oil)

AGRODOLCE

1 small red onion, thinly sliced

Extra-virgin olive oil

5 or 6 fresh sage leaves

1 tablespoon fresh rosemary
leaves

¼ cup honey

¼ cup red wine vinegar

¼ cup warm water

1. Equally stagger two racks in the oven and preheat it to 450°F. Line two sheet pans with parchment paper.

2. Cook the quinoa according to the package directions and set aside.

3. Spread the kale evenly on one of the lined sheet pans and the cabbage on the other pan. Drizzle both with the avocado oil, season with salt and a few cracks of black pepper, and mix to coat. Roast the cabbage on the bottom rack until charred on the edges and slightly crisp, 20 to 23 minutes. For the last 5 to 7 minutes of baking, add the kale to the top rack. Remove both pans from the oven and reduce the oven temperature to 375°F.

4. Spread the quinoa on a sheet pan and drizzle the chili oil all over. Season with ¼ teaspoon salt and mix. Roast the quinoa on the top rack until it is golden and lightly crisp, 19 to 21 minutes, stirring halfway through.

5. Meanwhile, make the agrodolce: Place the onion in a small heatproof bowl.

6. Set a small saucepan over medium heat and add 1 tablespoon olive oil. Add the sage and rosemary and sizzle for 1 to 2 minutes.

7. In a small bowl, whisk together the honey, vinegar, and water. Pour the honey-vinegar mixture into the pan, season with salt, and bring to a simmer. Let the mixture simmer for 2 to 3 minutes to thicken. Remove the sage and rosemary and pour the mixture over the red onion. Stir to combine.

8. In a large bowl, mix together the kale and cabbage and dress with the red onion agrodolce. Pile generously into individual bowls and top each with the chili quinoa.

KALE SALAD WITH PRESERVED LEMON & PECORINO

Serves 4 as a side

This kale salad eats like a deconstructed pesto, with pistachios instead of pine nuts to add a nice sweetness that plays up the brininess of the preserved lemon. I prefer the waxy deep green of Lacinato kale in this salad, but it works with other kale varieties just as well. The secret to this (and all kale salads) is to massage the kale at the beginning to mellow out its bite. But the upside to its hardiness is that it holds up for a few days, so you can have leftover salad that is actually worth eating again tomorrow.

1 bunch Lacinato kale (8 ounces), thinly sliced

2 tablespoons fresh lemon juice (about 1 lemon)

Extra-virgin olive oil

½ preserved lemon, homemade (see page 39) or store-bought

2 garlic cloves, grated

1 cup fresh basil leaves, chiffonade cut (see page 30)

½ cup roasted, salted pistachios

1 ounce Pecorino Romano cheese

Diamond Crystal kosher salt

Freshly ground black pepper

1. Add the kale to a large bowl. Drizzle with the lemon juice and 1 tablespoon olive oil and massage it into the kale for 1 to 2 minutes. Set the bowl aside.

2. Finely chop the preserved lemon into almost a paste. Add this and the garlic to the bottom of a second large bowl. Add the basil and kale and give everything a mix. Chop the pistachios as finely as possible (think: bread crumbs) and add them to the bowl. Grate in the Pecorino (I use Olive Garden rules: stop whenever you're ready), drizzle in 1 tablespoon olive oil, and mix again. Taste and season with salt and black pepper, as needed, but it shouldn't need much.

CELERY SALAD
WITH HUNKS OF PARMESAN

Serves 4 to 6 as a side

This is the kind of salad you could serve me at a restaurant, and I would talk about it for days afterward, without ever knowing how little goes into it. Crisp and mellowed red onion, chunks of sticky dates, torn mint, and salty Parm are all that carries this, with the thinnest celery slices as the vehicle. As a converted celery skeptic, I've learned that its flavor can vary hugely, based on where you buy it. This is one vegetable where if you can buy it from a farmers' market whole with leaves still intact, usually in midsummer to fall, it will be infinitely better than the kind you find wrapped in plastic at the store.

½ medium red onion, thinly sliced

½ bunch celery (1 pound), leaves reserved, stalks thinly sliced on an angle

4 or 5 large Medjool dates, pitted and chopped

15 to 20 fresh mint leaves, chiffonade cut (see page 30)

2 garlic cloves, grated

1 teaspoon grated lemon zest (about ½ lemon)

3 tablespoons fresh lemon juice (about 1 lemon)

1 tablespoon white wine vinegar, plus more to taste

Diamond Crystal kosher salt

Freshly ground black pepper

Extra-virgin olive oil

2 ounces Parmesan cheese

1 . Set up a bowl of ice and water and add the red onion. Let it sit for 5 to 10 minutes to get mellow and crisp.

2 . In a large bowl, combine the celery leaves, sliced celery, dates, and mint. Drain the red onion and add to the bowl. Add the garlic, lemon zest and juice, and vinegar. Season with ½ teaspoon salt and a few cracks of black pepper. Taste before adding 1 to 2 tablespoons olive oil. Stir, taste, and season with more salt, oil, or vinegar, as needed.

3 . Use a vegetable peeler to peel in the Parmesan in big strips. Toss again and serve.

BASIL CUCUMBERS
WITH SLIGHTLY SWEET PEANUTS

Serves 4 as a side

I am an absolute sucker for when two types of crunch line up *perfectly* together—salads are just a texture experiment after all—and that's exactly what this cucumber plus peanut concoction feels like. The peanuts have a densely crunchy Nutz for Nutz quality to them (aka, those small carts around New York City that sell candied nuts and smell *incredible*), while the smashed cucumber adds a fresh, cold crunch that makes this whole thing crunchy times one thousand. Plus, I know this calls for Thai basil, but if Italian basil is all you have, that will work, too.

3 large cucumbers

Diamond Crystal kosher salt

⅓ cup raw peanuts, coarsely chopped

1 tablespoon brown sugar

1 teaspoon sriracha

1 teaspoon toasted sesame oil

1 tablespoon soy sauce

1 tablespoon rice vinegar

1 tablespoon fresh lime juice (about ½ lime)

½ cup fresh Thai basil leaves, roughly torn

¼ teaspoon gochugaru, for serving (optional)

1. Cut the cucumbers crosswise into four pieces each. Halve these pieces lengthwise, then use the side of your knife to gently smash the cucumbers, cracking the skin slightly. Remove any seeds that naturally fall away. Add the cucumber chunks to a fine-mesh sieve and sprinkle with ¼ teaspoon salt. Press down on the cucumbers with a heavy object (I like to use something like a frozen bag of vegetables or zip-seal bag filled with ice) and let the cucumbers sit for 15 to 30 minutes to drain off any excess liquid.

2. Set a medium sauté pan over medium heat and toast the peanuts until fragrant, about 3 minutes. Add the brown sugar, sriracha, sesame oil, and 1 tablespoon water and cook, stirring often, until the water bubbles off and the peanuts start to look sticky. Season with ¼ teaspoon salt. Remove the pan from the heat and let the peanuts harden for a few minutes.

3. In a large bowl, combine the cucumbers, soy sauce, vinegar, lime juice, and basil. Mix together. Spoon the sticky peanuts directly over the cucumbers. If desired, sprinkle with gochugaru before serving.

TAMARI HEIRLOOM TOMATOES

Serves 4 as a side

Heirloom tomatoes are good enough to eat with salt and nothing else . . . but sometimes a person can't resist a little *something* else. (And let's be honest: Not all farmers' market tomatoes are winners.) In this simple pile of tomatoes, I've swapped the salt for umami-packed tamari, which brings out the best of the tomatoes without overpowering their sweet juiciness. The garlic-ginger-tamari dressing soaks into the fruits' crevices, so spooning the tomato juices from the bowl is strongly encouraged.

2 scallions

¼ cup sliced almonds

3 garlic cloves, grated

1 tablespoon grated
fresh ginger

2 Thai red chilies, seeded
and finely chopped

2 tablespoons tamari or
soy sauce

1 tablespoon rice vinegar

1 tablespoon honey

2 teaspoons toasted sesame oil

3 medium heirloom tomatoes

2 teaspoons chili crisp,
for serving (optional)

1. In a small bowl, prepare an ice bath. Thinly slice the scallions on an angle, then transfer them to the ice bath to crisp up.

2. Set a pan over medium heat and toast the almonds until golden and fragrant, 4 to 5 minutes. Remove from the pan and set aside to cool.

3. In a large bowl, combine the garlic, ginger, chilies, tamari, vinegar, honey, and sesame oil. Whisk to combine and let sit for 5 to 10 minutes to let the flavors meld into one another.

4. Cut the tomatoes into big, juicy wedges. Add them to the bowl and gently mix to coat them in the sauce. Drain and dry the scallions before adding them, along with the toasted almonds.

5. Mix everything together and transfer to a serving plate. If a little extra heat is desired, dot with chili crisp.

A SPOON SALAD

Serves 4

Consider this a love letter to underripe avocado, an underutilized, highly delicious food that is built on impatience. *And I love when I get to be impatient.* Underripe avocados have a pleasantly toothsome bite, a slight herbaceous tone, and they hold their shape when tossed in a salad with other teeny, tiny scoopable pieces. Enter scene: a Spoon Salad, a salad that's piled with herbs, golden-seared Halloumi, barely browned cauliflower, chewy farro, and a spicy-sticky dressing. Make it ahead if you want lunch for the week or serve it for a group. This colorful mix of cheese, grains, and veg will be a favorite in either scenario.

1 cup farro

1 small head cauliflower (1½ pounds)

5 ounces Halloumi cheese

Extra-virgin olive oil

Diamond Crystal kosher salt

2 Thai red chilies, seeded and thinly sliced

½ small red onion, thinly sliced

¾ cup red wine vinegar

¼ cup honey

¼ cup golden raisins, chopped

1 medium underripe avocado

1 cup tender fresh herbs, such as parsley, mint, dill, cilantro

1 . Cook the farro according to the package directions and set aside.

2 . Chop the cauliflower into small pieces, each no bigger than a bean. Cube the Halloumi into equally small pieces.

3 . Set a large pan over medium heat and add 2 tablespoons olive oil. Add the cauliflower and cook, stirring occasionally, until some pieces are darkened, 7 to 10 minutes. Season with a few pinches of salt and add to the bowl with the farro.

4 . Add another 1 tablespoon olive oil to the pan and add the Halloumi. Cook, undisturbed, for 2 minutes to get a nice sear on one side, then shake the Halloumi around and cook for another 1 to 2 minutes to give everything a bit more color. Transfer to the bowl with the farro.

5 . Set the pan back over medium heat and add the chilies, onion, vinegar, honey, and raisins. Bring to a simmer and let reduce until syrupy, 8 to 9 minutes.

6 . While the dressing reduces, cube the avocado into small pieces and tear the herbs. Add both to the bowl with the farro. Mix to combine, taste, and season with salt, as needed.

7 . When the golden raisin dressing is finished, let it cool to room temperature, then pour it over the salad and mix. Serve immediately.

SPRING PEAS & EDAMAME WITH GREENY TAHINI

Serves 4

I had a few good years, post college, where bags of frozen edamame sustained me. Edamame on rice with soy sauce was my dinner at least three times a week when I was working as an assistant, and I still think it's one of the best three-ingredient meals on the planet. I've since graduated to using edamame in different ways, with this green and garlicky tahini being one of my favorites. It eats well with some fresh spring peas, which I keep raw, crispy, and sweet, especially since they're matched up against such a salty and creamy dressing. Every now and then I make this salad with rice to relive my assistant days, just, y'know, this time without the two roommates.

2 pounds sugar snap peas

2 cups shelled edamame

1 lemon

8 flat anchovy fillets, packed in oil

2 garlic cloves, grated

½ cup tahini

½ cup fresh parsley leaves

Diamond Crystal kosher salt

Extra-virgin olive oil

⅔ cup Sourdough Bread Crumbs (page 46)

NOTE: You may have some dressing left over. Store it in the fridge for up to 5 days and use it on eggs, toast, sandwiches, pasta salads, as a dip for vegetables, you get it—it's versatile!

1. Trim and clean the sugar snap peas, then slice them on a sharp diagonal into two or three pieces.

2. In a bowl, combine the sugar snaps and edamame. Grate in about 1 teaspoon lemon zest. Halve the lemon and squeeze to get 3 tablespoons and set aside. (Set the lemon halves aside, too, for serving.)

3. Set a small sauté pan over medium-low heat and warm 1 teaspoon of the oil from the anchovy tin or jar. Drop in the anchovies and cook, stirring constantly, until they "melt" into the oil, separating into anchovy paste. Add the garlic, increase the heat to medium, and cook for a minute or so until the garlic is no longer raw (but don't let it burn). Transfer this mixture to a blender and add the tahini, lemon juice, parsley, and ½ cup cool water. Blend for a few seconds, just long enough to get the parsley mostly combined but still with a few green flecks throughout. Taste and season with a pinch of salt, as needed.

4. Place the same pan back over medium heat. Add 2 tablespoons olive oil and the bread crumbs. Toast for 3 to 4 minutes or until the bread crumbs are golden brown. Season with a pinch of salt and set aside.

5. Pour a half cup of the dressing over the peas and edamame and mix together, adding more to taste. Divide among four bowls and top with a handful of bread crumbs. Grate in any lemon zest remaining on the reserved lemon halves.

CITRUS-GINGER CABBAGE WITH SESAME TOFU

Makes 4 (big!) salads

This is the salad that wakes me up from my cozy-soups-and-stews hibernation that usually occurs between the months of November and February. The dressing is gingery and bright, taking full advantage of the best of the winter citrus season. The sesame-sizzled tofu is what makes this salad a meal, with a nutty, toasty crunch that plays off the sweet cabbage. This also works wonderfully with chicories, which I know from experience, since in the colder months when chicories are at their prime, I have this salad on repeat.

½ cup cashews

Boiling water

1 medium head red cabbage (2 pounds)

1 medium Cara Cara orange

½ teaspoon grated lime zest (about ½ lime)

1 tablespoon fresh lime juice (about ½ lime)

½ cup fresh cilantro leaves, plus a few sprigs for garnish

1 tablespoon grated fresh ginger

3 garlic cloves, grated

1 tablespoon soy sauce

1 tablespoon rice vinegar

½ teaspoon sriracha

½ cup fresh mint leaves, plus a few leaves for garnish

1 (16-ounce) block extra-firm tofu

2 teaspoons toasted sesame oil

Diamond Crystal kosher salt

Avocado oil

1 tablespoon white sesame seeds

1. Put the cashews in a small heatproof bowl and add boiling water to cover. Set aside.

2. Thinly slice the cabbage with a knife or on a mandoline and place in a large bowl. Supreme the orange (see opposite) and add the segments to the cabbage. Squeeze any juice from the leftover orange peels over the cabbage. Add the lime zest.

3. In a blender, combine the center piece of the orange (no waste!), lime juice, ¼ cup of the cilantro, the ginger, garlic, soy sauce, vinegar, and sriracha. Drain the cashews and add them to the blender with ½ cup cool water. Blend until smooth, adding a bit more water if it's too thick.

4. Pour this dressing over the cabbage and stir to combine. Tear in the remaining cilantro and all the mint.

5. Cut the tofu into 1-inch-thick squares and press out any moisture (see page 207). In a large bowl, gently toss the tofu pieces with the sesame oil and a pinch of salt.

6. Set a large pan over medium heat and add enough avocado oil to coat the bottom. Bring the oil up to 325°F and pan-fry the tofu pieces for 3 to 4 minutes on each side. When the tofu is finished remove it from the pan, turn the heat to medium-low, add the sesame seeds, and toast until golden brown, 3 to 4 minutes.

7. Pile the salad into a bowl, add the tofu on top, and garnish with the toasted sesame seeds and a few mint and cilantro leaves.

REIGN SUPREME

To "supreme" is to cut out the juicy, center piece of an orange slice, leaving the pith and peel behind. Start with a sharp knife and slice off the ends of the fruit, revealing the flesh. Stand the fruit on a flat end and glide your knife from the top to the bottom, cutting off the rind and pith but removing as little flesh as possible. There might be some flesh still on there, but that's okay.

Then hold the peeled fruit in your hand and use a paring knife to slice down both sides of a fruit slice, skimming the membranes. When your cuts meet at the bottom, it will free the slice, or the supreme, as we now call it. Do this over a bowl to catch any juices and supreme away.

BLISTERED SHISHITO PEPPERS
IN LEMON-JALAPEÑO DRESSING

Serves 4 to 6 as a side

I served a version of this salad on crostini at a party, and the one thing I kept hearing was how people had never had shishito peppers prepared this way before—probably because the way we usually encounter them in restaurants is blistered and whole. I'm a big fan of slicing and sautéing them, ever since stumbling upon the technique in one of the 987 (give or take) recipes I cooked, after I rescued *The Essential New York Times Cookbook* from someone's stoop. The sliced shishitos—seeds and all—have a gentle, green heat that's amped up by a lemony jalapeño dressing. To top it off, one of my favorite ingredients, crackly buckwheat groats, brings some much-needed crunch, but if you're craving some protein, Crumbled Chickpeas (page 40) would be great here, too.

Extra-virgin olive oil

1¼ pounds shishito peppers, stems removed

Diamond Crystal kosher salt

½ cup buckwheat groats

2 jalapeños, seeded and finely diced

1 shallot, finely diced

2 garlic cloves, grated

1 teaspoon grated lemon zest (about ½ lemon)

2 tablespoons fresh lemon juice (about 1 lemon)

½ cup fresh mint leaves, torn

½ cup fresh basil leaves, torn

1 . Set a large pan over medium heat and add 1 tablespoon olive oil. Add the shishito peppers to the pan and cook, flipping occasionally, until blistered, 5 to 6 minutes. Transfer them to a cutting board and when they are cool enough to handle, cut them crosswise into thin slices. Transfer them to a large bowl and season with a pinch of salt.

2 . Add the buckwheat groats to the pan and toast, stirring often, until the buckwheat has darkened in color and smells nutty and fragrant, 3 to 4 minutes. Remove them from the pan and set aside.

3 . To a small bowl, add the jalapeños, shallot, garlic, lemon zest and juice. Add 2 tablespoons olive oil and ½ teaspoon salt. Stir and season to taste. Pour this dressing over the peppers, then add the mint and basil. Give a few big mixes to combine.

4 . Scoop the salad onto a serving plate and top with the buckwheat groats right before serving.

QUITE THE PAIR

Mint and basil are used together in the Blistered Shishito Peppers in Lemon-Jalapeño Dressing (page 129). You can see they're used together in other recipes, too—Fava Beans with Preserved Lemon Ricotta (page 171), for example. And that's because they're one of my tried-and-true pairings. I call them partner ingredients—groups of things that work well together more often than not.

I tried to write a guide to pairings for this book but quickly realized the flaws in that endeavor. First, there's an entire (and very famous) book, *The Flavor Bible*, which is wholly dedicated to the subject of food pairing, and second, ingredients that go together are hardly prescriptive. Basil and mint might be a great pair here, but if they ended up in, say, a brown sugar cobbler, they might not be as compatible (okay . . . that *could* work . . . but let's pretend it doesn't for this argument!).

But finding and identifying pairings is how I started to build my recipe roster. It first clicked when I read through a favorite cookbook and saw the chef repeated the grouping of lemon, basil, mint, and Pecorino more than once. I

started to draw more parallels between other ingredients I saw used together, in that book and others. As I connected the dots, more and more partner ingredients emerged. To point you to examples in this book, I often pair red wine vinegar and honey (see Baked Kale Salad with Chili Quinoa, page 113, and Rosemary-Vinegared Mushrooms, page 136, and A Spoon Salad, page 122), tomatoes and chilies (Tamari Heirloom Tomatoes, page 121, and Hot Tomato Spread, page 86), and, of course, basil and mint.

I'm not saying you need to be on the lookout for pairings at all times, but as you cook, you might find partner ingredients of your own.

The more conscious you are of partner ingredients, the faster you can build meals without a full recipe, because you'll be able to rely on them to bring the flavor you're looking for and already have a feel for the result. (And that's why I'm going through a lot of red wine vinegar and honey these days!) As you eat through this book and others, watch for all these reliable combinations. They aren't there by accident.

CHILLED CHILI POTATOES, TOMATOES, OLIVES & CUCUMBERS

Serves 4

This salad is one of the reasons I always have boiled potatoes just hanging out in my fridge. That's normal, right? Cold potatoes are deeply underrated, but we're changing that one potato(ish) salad at a time. Here, lightly smashed potatoes provide a starchy, creamy contrast to the bright, crisp vegetables, making this salad equal parts hearty and refreshing. The lemony dill dressing is something I fall back on again and again, since I always seem to (also) have yogurt, lemon, and dill in my fridge. Adding a jammy egg makes this niçoise-adjacent, which makes me feel fancy and très chic.

Diamond Crystal kosher salt

1 pound white baby potatoes

4 large eggs

½ small sweet onion, thinly sliced

1 pound (1 pint) cherry tomatoes, assorted colors, halved

3 ounces (about ½ cup) pitted green olives, chopped

4 Persian (mini) cucumbers, quartered lengthwise and sliced

¼ cup fresh basil leaves, torn

½ cup fresh dill, chopped

Freshly ground black pepper

1 teaspoon grated lemon zest (about ½ lemon)

3 tablespoons fresh lemon juice (about 1 lemon)

¼ cup whole-milk yogurt

2 garlic cloves, grated

¼ teaspoon red pepper flakes

Extra-virgin olive oil

2 teaspoons Calabrian chili oil

1. Set a large pot of water over high heat and bring to a boil. Add 1 tablespoon salt to the water, then add the potatoes and boil until fork-tender, 12 to 16 minutes. Use a slotted spoon (don't drain that water!) to transfer the potatoes to a bowl. Transfer the bowl to the fridge to chill.

2. Add the eggs to the still-boiling water and boil for 6 minutes. While the eggs are boiling, prepare an ice bath. Transfer the eggs to the ice bath when they are finished boiling.

3. Add the onion to another small bowl of ice water and let them soak for 5 minutes to make them wonderfully mellow and crisp. This is optional, but not really.

4. In a large bowl, combine the tomatoes, olives, cucumbers, basil, and ¼ cup of the dill. Drain and add the onions, season with salt and black pepper and mix.

5. In a small bowl, combine the remaining ¼ cup dill, the lemon zest and juice, yogurt, garlic, pepper flakes, and 2 tablespoons olive oil. Whisk together and season with ¼ teaspoon salt. Add a few spoonfuls of the dressing to the vegetables and mix. You want it lightly dressed, not gloopy.

6. Pull the potatoes out of the fridge and rough them up with a wooden spoon, gently smashing and tearing some pieces to get a rough surface area. Add the chili oil and a few pinches of salt and toss.

7. To serve, divide the tomato salad among four serving plates and top with a portion of the potatoes. Peel and halve the eggs, adding one to each dish. Drizzle with the remaining dressing before serving.

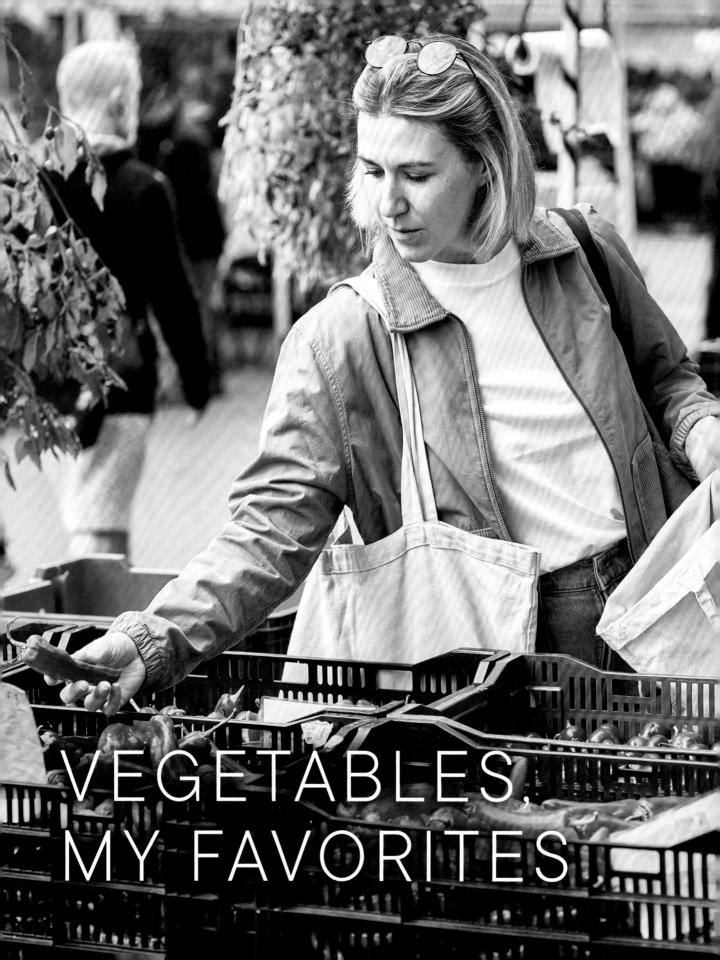

VEGETABLES,
MY FAVORITES

WHEN I FIRST STARTED COOKING, I was hyperfocused on cabbage. I could get it for $2 a head (those were the days), and I'd sauté it into a wilty braise, over and over . . . and over. Maybe my cabbage overload is why there's only one cabbage recipe in this chapter (and it's not *the* braise, don't worry!), but what my cabbage repetition taught me is that you can build flavor *around* a vegetable, as well as *through* how you cook it. What I mean is that while I grew up hoping a sauce would cover up the blah taste of my steamed green beans, now I can see how the sizzled mint on page 140 pairs with frizzled beans' charred edges and subtly sweet interior.

I also noticed that many cooks often focus on main proteins for dinner, while the side is roasted vegetables, dutifully tossed in the oven. What if we swapped that? So, in this chapter, we have standout vegetable dishes that I often make as a side to a simpler main, like a pan-fried piece of salt-and-pepper salmon. Each vegetable is matched with a technique to bring out its best texture and flavor, but the sauces and dressings are so versatile that I hope you pick up a few to take with you into many other vegetable endeavors.

ROSEMARY-VINEGARED MUSHROOMS

Serves 4 as a side

My mushroom epiphany happened in front of a pan, the first time I witnessed an oyster mushroom flip, sizzle, and seize up into a crispy golden brown. I've since learned that to get a mushroom to the level of potato-chip crisp, patience is key. You have to pull out the moisture first, then continue to hit them with high heat. While these mushrooms are oven roasted, the same rules apply. They come out super light and crunchy, their deep umami is enlivened with vinegar and herbs, and everything's set over a swipe of garlicky yogurt. It's a proper side dish, but if you don't think you can eat a whole oyster mushroom in one sitting . . . just you wait.

1 garlic head

Extra-virgin olive oil

½ pound oyster mushrooms, very well cleaned

Diamond Crystal kosher salt

1 tablespoon fresh rosemary

5 or 6 fresh sage leaves

Freshly ground black pepper

2 tablespoons white wine vinegar

1 tablespoon honey

¼ cup Cashew Cream (page 39), yogurt, or ricotta cheese

1 . Position a rack in the center of the oven and preheat to 425°F. Line a sheet pan with parchment paper.

2 . Slice off the top third of the garlic head to expose the cloves and drizzle with 1 tablespoon olive oil. Wrap in aluminum foil (or follow the instructions on page 45) and roast it until soft, about 40 to 45 minutes.

3 . At the same time, peel the mushroom into small strips, following the lines of the base. Toss with 2 tablespoons olive oil and season with ¼ teaspoon salt before scattering on the lined sheet pan and transferring to the oven. Roast until they are a dark, golden crisp, 20 to 22 minutes.

4 . While the mushrooms are roasting, set a small sauté pan over medium heat and add 1 tablespoon olive oil, the rosemary, and sage and cook, undisturbed, until the rosemary is dark and the sage has crisped up, 2 to 3 minutes. Season with a pinch of salt and a few cracks of black pepper, then pour in the vinegar and honey. Stir to combine and let this mixture simmer until the vinegar has reduced by half and everything is syrupy, 4 to 5 minutes.

5 . In a small bowl, mix together the cashew cream and a pinch of salt. Squeeze in the roasted garlic cloves and mix well.

6 . When the mushrooms are out of the oven, spoon the vinegar and herb mixture over them and toss so that the mushrooms are lightly dressed. Swipe the garlicky cashew cream on the bottom of a plate and pile the mushrooms on top.

TEMPURA-FRIED ASPARAGUS WITH BUTTERMILK DRESSING

Serves 4 as a side

I promise that I love asparagus roasted and blanched and grilled, and *I do*. But I really, *really* love it fried. Shape-wise, asparagus is the au naturel fry! It's also strong enough to hold some bite after frying, and quick enough that you can do a few batches in 10 minutes while someone else mixes the drinks—asparagus is the ideal cocktail snack. If you're not the biggest fan of shallow frying for fear of, well, sizzling oil right next to your fingers, do not fear: Use a big pan with high sides and then get your hands on an instant-read thermometer, so you can keep the oil between 325° and 350°F, which should keep everything stable and not so scary.

1 large egg

1 cup / 234ml ice water

1 cup / 140g all-purpose flour

Diamond Crystal kosher salt

Avocado oil

1 pound asparagus spears, 2 inches of stem end removed

½ cup / 120ml buttermilk

1 teaspoon grated lemon zest (about ½ lemon)

2 tablespoons fresh lemon juice (about 1 lemon)

2 garlic cloves, grated

¼ cup / 15g chopped fresh dill, chives, or mixture of both

Freshly ground black pepper

1 teaspoon chili oil (I prefer Calabrian chili oil or Brightland Ardor oil), for serving

1 teaspoon black sesame seeds, for serving

1 . In a large bowl, beat together the egg and ice water. Add the flour and 1 teaspoon salt and whisk to combine into a smooth batter.

2 . Set a large high-sided sauté pan over medium heat and pour in ½ inch of avocado oil. Heat the oil to 325° to 350°F on an instant-read thermometer.

3 . Working with three or four spears at a time, dip each asparagus spear in the batter and very gently place into the oil. Fry until golden, 3 to 4 minutes, gently flipping halfway through. I like these on the darker side compared to your average tempura. Transfer to a paper towel and repeat until all the spears are cooked.

4 . In a small bowl, whisk together the buttermilk, lemon zest and juice, garlic, and dill. Season with a generous pinch of salt and a few cracks of black pepper. Taste and add more salt, as needed.

5 . To serve, add a big swipe of the buttermilk dressing to the bottom of a plate and place the asparagus on top. Top with more dressing, dot with the chili oil, and sprinkle with the sesame seeds. Alternatively, you can dot the chili oil on top of a bowl of the dressing and serve the asparagus on a plate to the side, for more of a finger food, dipping situation.

FRIZZLED GREEN BEANS WITH SIZZLED SESAME & MINT

Serves 4

A nearly charred green bean is a thing of beauty. But let's call it frizzling, so it doesn't sound as if I'm telling you to nearly burn something, okay? By frizzling our green beans, we're able to coax out a smoky char and find the sweetness that hides inside of those waxy green shells. After the frizzle, I use the pan to quickly sizzle some sesame seeds and dried mint into a sweet but crunchy coating. It's frizzle meets sizzle, leaving you with a punchy, nutty pile of beans.

Extra-virgin olive oil

1½ pounds green beans, ends trimmed

Diamond Crystal kosher salt

3 tablespoons white sesame seeds

2 teaspoons coriander pods, crushed

2 teaspoons dried mint

¼ teaspoon red pepper flakes

1 teaspoon honey

1 teaspoon sherry vinegar or red wine vinegar

2 tablespoons pickled red onions, homemade (see page 49) or store-bought

1. Set a large pan over medium heat and add 1 tablespoon olive oil. In two batches, frizzle the green beans for 3 minutes, before flipping and cooking until dark spots appear all over, an additional 3 to 4 minutes, adding another tablespoon of olive oil before you cook the next batch. Season with a pinch of salt and set aside.

2. Turn the heat to medium-low and add 3 tablespoons olive oil. Add the sesame seeds and cook, stirring occasionally, until golden, 3 to 5 minutes. When the sesame seeds are golden and fragrant, add the coriander, mint, and pepper flakes and stir to combine. Turn off the heat, add the honey and vinegar, and swirl everything together. Season with ¼ teaspoon salt, plus more to taste.

3. Add the green beans back to the pan and mix to coat them in the seedy mixture. Pour this onto a serving plate, scraping any remaining sesame mixture on top. Scatter the green beans with the pickled red onions and serve.

GREENER ZUCCHINI GRATIN

Serves 6

In summer, among the mix of tomato salads and watermelon spears, I start to crave what I dub summer comfort. Easy, filling, heartier recipes. Enter scene: green zucchini gratin, which you can do with either zucchini or those bright yellow summer squashes that cook down into the same soft, melty texture. There's no cheese in this gratin, but cream mingles with bread crumbs and bright green basil oil in a way that gets all smooth and pesto-pasta reminiscent.

2 pounds zucchini, summer squash, or a mixture of both, sliced into thin medallions

¼ cup basil herb oil (see Your Perfect Herb Oil, page 34)

⅔ cup heavy cream

Diamond Crystal kosher salt

2 cups Sourdough Bread Crumbs (page 46)

¼ cup fresh basil leaves

Freshly ground black pepper

1. Position a rack in the center of the oven and preheat it to 375°F.

2. In a large bowl, combine the zucchini and basil oil. Do a few big mixes so the medallions are coated, then mix in the cream. Season with salt.

3. In a food processor, pulse together the bread crumbs and basil for 30 seconds to a minute, until all the basil is chopped into the same size as the bread crumbs.

4. In a 8 by 8-inch baking dish, spread out half the zucchini in an even layer. Add 1 cup of the bread crumbs on top, then top with the remaining zucchini. Pour over any remaining cream from the bowl. Top with the remaining 1 cup bread crumbs and add a few cracks of black pepper.

5. Bake until the cream at the edges is beginning to turn a golden brown, 40 to 50 minutes. If you notice your bread crumbs are getting a touch too brown, tent the pan with aluminum foil.

6. When it's out of the oven, wait until it's no longer bubbling, then serve warm.

STICKY, MELTY FAIRY TALE EGGPLANT WITH SCALLIONS & MINT

Serves 4 as a side

My two favorite condiments make an appearance in this recipe, doing what they do best: being all sticky, spicy, and sweet. Indonesian kecap manis, a sweet soy sauce, and sambal oelek, a fermented hot sauce, coat this melty, creamy eggplant, and I'm salivating just typing about it. I can't resist those cute fairy tale eggplants, but a long, Japanese-style eggplant will also work. This is also a fun recipe to throw on the grill, and if you're grilling other vegetables, you can always double the sauce and share the love.

1½ pounds fairy tale eggplants

Diamond Crystal kosher salt

1 tablespoon white sesame seeds

Extra-virgin olive oil

3 tablespoons kecap manis

2 tablespoons sambal oelek

2 scallions, thinly sliced

15 fresh mint leaves, roughly torn

1 . Remove the tops from the eggplants (don't worry, they'll still be cute) and halve them lengthwise. Lightly score the flesh in a crisscross pattern, being sure not to cut too deep. Season each cut side with a pinch of salt and let them sit for 5 to 10 minutes, then pat off any moisture droplets with a paper towel.

2 . Set a large pan over medium heat and toast the sesame seeds until golden, 4 to 5 minutes. Transfer the seeds to a small bowl.

3 . Add 2 tablespoons olive oil to the pan. Working in batches, add the eggplants cut-side down first, and cook until darkened and soft, 3 to 4 minutes per side. Transfer to a plate. Add more olive oil as needed for subsequent batches, since eggplants soak up oil like a sponge.

4 . When the eggplants are caramelized all over, leave the last batch in the pan, turn off the heat, and add the kecap manis and sambal oelek. Cook for only a minute, stirring together so the two sauces combine. Toss all the eggplant back in and stir into a sticky pile.

5 . Serve topped with the sesame seeds, scallions, and mint.

CAULIFLOWER WITH COCONUT DRESSING & FRESNO ALMONDS

Serves 4 to 6 as a side

I like my floret-family vegetables (broccoli, cauliflower, Romanesco, you get it) with a lighter sauce, and this coconut milk dressing perfectly coats a hard-roasted cauliflower without weighing it down. The almonds are toasted in a quick Fresno pepper oil, making them salty, spicy, and a dynamite combo alongside the pops of sweet cherries. It's a roasted vegetable dish, but it still feels light and refreshing, with texture and flavor that keep your mouth guessing.

1 head cauliflower (2 pounds)

Extra-virgin olive oil

Diamond Crystal kosher salt

1 Fresno pepper, seeded and halved

1 garlic clove, grated

1 teaspoon grated lime zest (about ½ lime)

2 tablespoons fresh lime juice (about 1 lime)

¼ cup canned unsweetened full-fat coconut milk

½ cup fresh mint leaves

½ cup fresh cilantro leaves

1 teaspoon sugar

⅓ cup raw almonds

1½ cups sweet cherries (½ pound), pitted and halved

1 . Position a rack in the center of the oven and preheat it to 450°F.

2 . Cut the cauliflower into cherry-size florets and spread them out on an unlined sheet pan. Drizzle with 2 tablespoons olive oil and season with a few big pinches of salt.

3 . Roast for 15 minutes, then give the pan a shake to flip the florets. Roast until the cauliflower has browned and crisped on the edges, another 10 to 15 minutes; don't be afraid to go dark.

4 . Meanwhile, finely dice half of the Fresno pepper and add it to a small bowl. Cut the other half into thin slices and set aside.

5 . To the bowl with the diced Fresno pepper, add the garlic, lime zest and juice, coconut milk, 5 finely chopped mint leaves, 1 tablespoon finely chopped cilantro, the sugar, and ½ teaspoon salt. Whisk this together and chill the dressing in the fridge while the cauliflower finishes roasting.

6 . Set a small pan over medium heat and add 2 tablespoons olive oil. Add the thinly sliced Fresno pepper and swirl, letting the oil simmer for 2 to 3 minutes. Add the almonds and let them toast in the oil until fragrant, another 2 to 3 minutes. Turn off the heat and season with salt.

7 . When the cauliflower is out of the oven, let it cool for a few minutes before adding it to a large bowl. Pour in the dressing and give it a few mixes. Add the cherries and almond–Fresno pepper mixture. Tear in the remaining mint and cilantro. Pile onto a big plate and serve.

ACV BRUSSELS SPROUTS IN TOASTED CORNMEAL

Serves 4 to 6 as a side

Aah, ACV, it stands for apple cider vinegar—one of my absolute favorite vinegars to cook with, although you don't see it in recipes as often as others (yet!). Its tangy brightness balances well with the earthiness of a Brussels sprout, especially when the sprout is thinly sliced and roasted to dark and crispy oblivion. Still, I enjoy adding a texture play of something crunchy on Brussels, so here I use toasted cornmeal. It toasts down with some melty red onion, and the resulting crumble topping gives this recipe an always-invited Thanksgiving feel.

1½ pounds Brussels sprouts, trimmed, halved, and thinly sliced

Extra-virgin olive oil

Diamond Crystal kosher salt

¼ cup apple cider vinegar

2 tablespoons honey

½ teaspoon red pepper flakes

Freshly ground black pepper

½ red onion, thinly sliced

½ cup yellow cornmeal

1 . Equally stagger two racks in the oven and preheat it to 425°F.

2 . Toss the sprouts with 2 tablespoons olive oil, season with a pinch of salt, and scatter on two sheet pans. Roast until the sprouts are tender and beginning to brown on the edges, 20 to 22 minutes.

3 . In a small bowl, whisk together the vinegar, honey, and pepper flakes and season with a pinch of salt and a few cracks of black pepper.

4 . Set a large pan over medium heat and add 2 tablespoons olive oil. Add the red onion, season with a pinch of salt, and cook, stirring occasionally, until softened, about 8 minutes.

5 . Add the cornmeal and toast until it's beginning to turn a deep golden brown, 7 to 8 minutes. Drizzle in 2 tablespoons of the vinegar mixture, turn off the heat, and shake the cornmeal into a crumble.

6 . When the sprouts are out of the oven, toss with the remaining vinegar mixture on the sheet pan. Transfer to a serving dish and scatter the cornmeal mixture over everything.

BLACKENED SQUASH IN TOMATO BROWN BUTTER

Serves 4 to 6 as a side

Using two types of winter squash is not necessary for this recipe, but it does make piling everything on a plate that much more satisfying, because each brings its own subtle flavor difference. But what's special is the tomato (brown!) butter, which is nutty and sweet, yet tangy and buttery all at once. The darker you let the butter get, the better, since you'll be rewarded with a rich, deep sauce that brings out the sweetness of the roasted squash.

1 large kabocha squash (2 pounds), or 2 smaller squashes, such as delicata, acorn, or honeynut

Extra-virgin olive oil

Diamond Crystal kosher salt

4 tablespoons salted butter

2 tablespoons tomato paste

2 tablespoons white wine vinegar

1 tablespoon honey

½ teaspoon ground cumin

1 teaspoon caraway seeds, crushed

¼ teaspoon red pepper flakes

Freshly ground black pepper

½ cup torn fresh dill

1. Equally stagger two racks in the oven and preheat it to 450°F.

2. Halve the squash through the stem and pull out the seeds. If using delicata, halve lengthwise and pull out the seeds. Cut the squash into pieces: 1-inch-thick wedges for the kabocha and acorn; ½-inch-thick slices crosswise for the honeynut. Cut the delicata crosswise into ½-inch-thick half-moons. Spread the squash onto two unlined sheet pans, making sure each piece makes contact with the pan. Drizzle each pan with 2 tablespoons olive oil and season with a few generous pinches of salt. Mix to coat.

3. Transfer the pans to the oven and roast until cooked through, 20 to 22 minutes.

4. While the squash is roasting, set a medium pan over medium heat and add the butter and let it brown: At first it will fully melt, then begin to fizz and foam for 2 to 3 minutes, forming dark brown flecks at the bottom of the pan. When it's a deep, amber brown color, after about 5 minutes, take the pan off the heat.

5. In a small bowl, whisk together the tomato paste, vinegar, honey, cumin, caraway seeds, pepper flakes, ¼ teaspoon black pepper, and ¼ cup water. Pour this into the brown butter and cook over medium heat for another 1 to 2 minutes, letting the tomato butter reduce by half, getting thick and almost syrupy. Taste and season with salt, as needed.

6. Pull the squash out of the oven, flip to reveal the charred brown undersides, and pour the tomato butter directly over the squash. Give a few gentle, big mixes to combine. The squash will be soft enough to break into pieces, which is fine and part of the appeal.

7. Garnish with the dill before serving and eat warm.

LIME-ROASTED CABBAGE
WITH TURMERIC WHITE BEAN MASH

Makes 4 (large) servings

This crispy-edged, limey cabbage holds a soft spot in my heart because, when I shared it online, everyone *loved* it, and it showed me how many people adore a fiber-y, unwieldly cabbage as much as I do. It's not hard to understand why, though—when you roast cabbage, it goes from rough and woody to tender and almost sweet, and the brown crispy edges it gets on a few rare pieces are gold. I pair it with a spice-packed white bean mash to make it a full meal, and nuggets of chewy rice are sprinkled over top, because I just can't help myself.

1 small head cabbage, red, savoy, or otherwise, thinly sliced (2 pounds)

Extra-virgin olive oil

Diamond Crystal kosher salt

¾ cup short-grain white rice

½ cup raw almonds

Boiling water

½ cup nutritional yeast

½ cup fresh cilantro leaves, rough bottom 2 inches of stems removed

2 garlic cloves

1 tablespoon sliced fresh ginger

1 teaspoon ground turmeric

½ teaspoon ground cumin

½ teaspoon Aleppo pepper flakes

½ teaspoon red pepper flakes

2 tablespoons apple cider vinegar

1 (15-ounce) can white beans, drained and rinsed

Avocado oil

1 tablespoon fresh lime juice (about 1 lime)

¼ cup tender fresh herbs, such as mint, basil, cilantro, for serving (optional)

1. Equally stagger two racks in the oven and preheat it to 400°F. Line two sheet pans with parchment paper.

2. Scatter the cabbage on the lined sheet pans. Drizzle each pan with 2 tablespoons olive oil and season with a few large pinches of salt. Mix to coat. Roast the cabbage until the edge pieces are golden brown, 20 to 22 minutes.

3. While the cabbage is roasting, cook the rice according to the package directions. (I like to use a rice cooker for this to keep everything simple.)

4. In a small heatproof bowl, cover the almonds with boiling-hot water and let soak for 5 minutes.

5. In a food processor, combine the nutritional yeast, cilantro, garlic, ginger, turmeric, cumin, Aleppo pepper flakes, red pepper flakes, and vinegar. Drain the almonds and add them to the food processor with ½ cup cool water and pulse until everything is roughly combined. Add the beans, season with ¼ teaspoon salt, and process until smooth. Taste, season, and set aside.

6. By this time, the rice should be finished. Set a large pan over medium heat and add enough avocado oil to coat the surface. When the oil reaches 325°F, add the rice in tablespoon-size chunks. Cook, undisturbed, until the rice is deeply golden on the bottom, 5 to 7 minutes. Use a slotted spoon to transfer the rice to a paper towel to drain.

7. When the cabbage is done roasting, squeeze the lime juice over it and mix. Taste and season with salt, as needed.

8. Plate the white bean mash, top with the cabbage, and sprinkle with rice nuggets. Top with the herbs, which are optional, but worth it if you have them.

ROASTED FENNEL WITH A MUSTARDY BALSAMIC

Serves 4 to 6 as a side

As fennel roasts, its intense licorice flavor mellows and gets completely sweet, while the fennel itself breaks down into some silky pieces, others more tender, and some almost crisp. It's a deeply underrated roasted vegetable, and it needs very little else to make it sing. I've found that a shiny balsamic dressing with two (yes, two, sorry!) kinds of mustard is just the thing to make this a phenomenal side dish. And if you're craving more crunch than these crispy fennel edges can give, the Sourdough Bread Crumbs (page 46) are there for you.

2 large fennel bulbs, stalks and fronds removed, cut into chunks

Extra-virgin olive oil

Diamond Crystal kosher salt

1 tablespoon smooth Dijon mustard

1 tablespoon whole-grain mustard

1 tablespoon honey

2 tablespoons balsamic vinegar

Freshly ground black pepper

1. Position a rack in the center of the oven and preheat it to 425°F.

2. Add the fennel to a sheet pan, drizzle with 2 tablespoons olive oil, and season with a few big pinches of salt. Mix to coat and spread out the fennel, being sure to give each piece plenty of room.

3. Roast the fennel until it is deeply brown and charred on the edges, 25 to 30 minutes.

4. While the fennel is roasting, in a medium bowl, whisk together both mustards, the honey, and vinegar. Whisking constantly, slowly pour in ¼ cup olive oil to make a creamy dressing. Taste and season with salt and black pepper, as needed.

5. When the fennel is out of the oven, transfer it to a serving dish and spoon over the dressing. Garnish with the fronds and additional cracks of black pepper.

FEEL-GOOD FOOD

A funny part of my story is I started as a health food blogger. You know, desserts made with only coconut sugar and cakes filled with substitutions for "bad" ingredients that never should have been labeled bad in the first place. It was a completely different time in my life, and I looked at food in a vastly different way. And while I've deviated far from that route, I still believe I cook healthily; it just means something else now.

If you've found this book because you know me, then you'll know my story. If you've found this book some other way (I'm *thrilled*, and *hello*), then all you need to know is that my history with food was not always easy-breezy, something I've found to be common among women in the food industry. Even chefs I admire the most, who sling rib eye steaks at their restaurants, or prolific food writers, who have built their lives around eating, have admitted that allowing themselves the same leisure, the same reckless abandon around food, has not always been easy. I am not the first woman to have a career in cooking but a bad history with eating, and while I wish it were different, I don't think I'll be the last.

But what I will say is that the first moment I allowed myself to relax around food—to dive into flavor and volume, variety and ingredients, to think of my meals as exploration without restriction—that's when my cooking changed. It didn't fit into a picture-perfect category of healthy (who even defines that term anymore?), but it became satisfying. It felt real in the way food never felt real before. Real butter, real vegetables, real cheese. And of course, foods that are processed, some by factories, some by me (because PS, even chopping a food makes it processed!). And I do still have people who ask me why I changed, why I "strayed," and all I can say is I found the food I believe in. It's part of building my food ethos, building the food that made my home. I like to cook with balance, with sugar, and with no judgment around how I eat it. Feeding people is what feeds me, but feeding myself feeds me, too. It's feel-good food.

BEANS, A FULL SENTENCE

I THINK IT'S OKAY TO SAY I HAVE A MILD BEAN OBSESSION.
A bean obsession lite, if you will. But that's because it's easy to fall in love with something so versatile, filling, and capable of soaking up flavor. Beans can be part of something or they can be the whole meal; that is why I call beans "the full sentence"— and I know it's cheesy (but PS, beans can also be!).

When I started cooking for myself and thinking in terms of complete meals—covering all my nutritional bases—beans, in their proteiny-carby state, became incredibly useful. Instead of a side dish, beans can be the texture maker, the base of a stew, the focus of a sauce, or the topping to a salad. They can go from crispy to creamy with just a few techniques, and their mild flavor assists everything you're cooking—not flavorless by far but not distinct enough to get in the way.

In this chapter, you'll find beans across a variety of applications, from rich and cheesy beans with orecchiette on page 163 to light and summery fava beans on page 171. I cook with both dried and canned beans, and the recipes work with both. (And if you haven't cooked with dried before, I'm here for you; see page 160.) All these dishes can be served, from start to finish, as a full meal. They'd also make killer sides if you're going that route, but on their own, these beans still qualify as the beginning, middle, and end of the sentence.

BASIC_BEANS

Makes 8 servings, or 6 cups of drained beans

At the writing of this book, my online username is Justine_Snacks, a name I jokingly chose when I first started cooking on the internet and the name that would carry me to the eventual writing of this recipe! The underscore, of course, is silent, and as an homage to my first username, I made sure Basic_Beans follows suit.

Dried beans are a tricky thing because no two bags are alike. The age, size, and variety of your beans all factor into the cooking time, so most bean recipes have to be pretty flexible. Luckily for me (and hopefully for you!), I've found a method I think is the simplest, most consistent way to make a large pot of basic, but also very delicious-on-their-own, beans. Yes, they do have to be soaked beforehand, but no, it's not the end of the world if you can only soak the morning of. You can eat them in their brothy, comforting state or, when drained and rinsed, use them as you would the canned version. If you're going that route, remember to save the flavorful cooking broth. I treat it like a really good chicken stock and use it in soups, to cook grains in, or (plot twist) to make more beans.

1 pound dried beans of choice (large white lima beans are my favorite)

Extra-virgin olive oil

1 small yellow onion, halved lengthwise

¼ teaspoon red pepper flakes

2 sprigs of fresh rosemary

1 bay leaf

1 head of garlic, halved crosswise

1 Parmesan cheese rind (optional, but delicious)

Diamond Crystal kosher salt

1. In a large Dutch oven or soup pot, combine the beans with water to cover by 2 inches; get ready for them to expand as they soak. Cover and soak for 6 hours or up to overnight. When you're ready to cook, drain the beans in a colander and rinse out the Dutch oven.

2. Return the beans to the pot and add 2 tablespoons olive oil, the onion, pepper flakes, rosemary, bay leaf, garlic, Parmesan rind (if using), and 10 cups water. Bring to a boil, then add 1 tablespoon salt. Turn the heat to a simmer, cover, and simmer for 30 minutes. Check for doneness and add another 1 tablespoon salt. Cover and cook until the beans are tender and creamy, without any shrively skin or tough bite, another 20 to 60 minutes, checking the bean's doneness every now and then. Note that the less time they have to soak, the longer they will take to cook. Remove the pot from the heat. Scoop out the onion, rosemary, bay leaf, garlic, and Parmesan rind (if using) and let cool before storing the beans in the fridge or freezer.

NOTE: Dried beans don't last forever, and while the beans in your pantry from three apartments ago are probably edible, you'll always get a better texture and taste from newer beans. I like heirloom beans, and if I'm in the mood to splurge, Rancho Gordo is a brand that's an easily accessible favorite. Cook your beans within 6 months for the best results . . . and definitely before that next apartment lease, okay?

BASIC_BEANS
WITH ORECCHIETTE & PARMESAN

Serves 8

One of my favorite uses for Basic_Beans is in this extra-comforting, extra-creamy pasta that you make right in the same pot as the beans during the last 15 minutes they are cooking. It's also easy to riff on. Any small pasta shape will do, and the greens could be anything from Swiss chard or thawed and drained frozen spinach. And I use Parmesan here, but sometimes I'm more in the mood for salty Pecorino or a nutty Gruyère. The cheese will melt right into the broth, which is why we reserve some for topping—because I would never leave you without the opportunity for a cheese-pull.

Basic_Beans (page 160)

1 pound orecchiette pasta

5 ounces Parmesan cheese, freshly grated (about 1⅓ cups)

3 cups kale, stems removed, coarsely chopped

Calabrian chili paste, for serving

Freshly ground black pepper

1. Follow the Basic_Beans recipe until the beans are 15 minutes away from being done. They'll be soft but will still have a slight al dente bite to them.

2. Remove the onion, rosemary, bay leaf, and garlic. Bring the pot of beans back to a gentle boil, add the orecchiette, and cook for 6 to 7 minutes. Set aside ½ cup of the Parmesan for serving. Turn the heat to medium-low. Add the rest of the Parmesan ½ cup at a time to the beans and stir constantly to let the cheese melt in with the pasta. The whole pot should begin to thicken.

3. When the cheese is fully combined in the pot, turn off the heat and add the kale. Stir to let the kale wilt into the pasta.

4. Scoop into individual bowls and dot on Calabrian chili paste to taste. Serve topped with some of the reserved Parmesan and black pepper.

BREADED BEANS WITH NUTTY SKHUG

Serves 4

Breaded beans are the closest thing we can get to fried beans, because actually frying beans is a recipe for explosion. Pure chaos. Not here, though! These creamy butter beans are coated in a crunchy, spicy breading and roasted until they poof (I'm sorry, but there's no other word for it). And if you've never "poofed" a bean, I invite you to try. It's very fulfilling. Some of your beans will pop open in the oven, which is nothing to worry about; in fact, it creates crispier, more craggily edges, and that means you're doing something right.

2 (15-ounce) cans butter beans, drained and rinsed

¼ cup whole-wheat flour

½ teaspoon garlic powder

¼ teaspoon ground nutmeg

¼ teaspoon chili powder

¼ teaspoon red pepper flakes

Diamond Crystal kosher salt

Freshly ground black pepper

Extra-virgin olive oil

NUTTY SKHUG

Spinachy Skhug (page 37)

3 tablespoons raw almonds

FOR SERVING

2 teaspoons grated lemon zest (about 1 lemon)

Extra-virgin olive oil

1 tablespoon fresh lemon juice

Toast, pita, or other dippable bread

1. Position a rack in the top of the oven and preheat it to 425°F. Line a sheet pan with parchment paper.

2. Place the rinsed butter beans (they should still be slightly damp) in a shallow bowl. Sprinkle with the flour, garlic powder, nutmeg, chili powder, and pepper flakes. Season with ½ teaspoon salt and many cracks of black pepper and toss to coat.

3. Transfer the coated beans to the lined sheet pan and spread them out in an even layer. Drizzle the beans with 2 tablespoons olive oil and gently toss on the pan. Roast the beans until they're golden brown and crisp, 22 to 25 minutes. Some will pop open, and that's a good thing!

4. While the beans are roasting, prepare the spinachy skhug as directed in the recipe, adding an additional 3 tablespoons almonds with the other ingredients to the food processor or blender to create an even thicker, spreadable sauce.

5. To serve, add a scoop of the nutty skhug to each plate and make a small indent in the center. Scatter the beans in the middle of the skhug. Top with the lemon zest and drizzle with some olive oil and the lemon juice. Serve with toast, pita, or whatever dippable bread you have on hand.

CINNAMON ROMESCO CHICKPEAS & CHARRED GREENS

Serves 4

This is a *messy* meal, which is fine by me, because life is messy. We've got crispy roasted chickpeas that share a sheet pan with kale, which then get smothered in a roasted red pepper and tomato romesco sauce that, like most sauces in this book, could really use a hunk of something bready for very-important-sauce-rescuing. The romesco's warm spices and the way the chickpeas always remain a little soft inside make this one of my favorite wintry dinners—best eaten at the table with a knife, fork, and napkin.

2 (15-ounce) cans chickpeas, drained and rinsed

Extra-virgin olive oil

Diamond Crystal kosher salt

Freshly ground black pepper

1 small red bell pepper, cored, seeded, and halved

1 medium globe tomato (Roma, San Marzano, or tomatoes on the vine work here, too)

2 garlic cloves, peeled but whole

3 tablespoons skin-on hazelnuts

½ teaspoon chili powder

½ teaspoon smoked paprika

¼ teaspoon ground cinnamon

¼ teaspoon red pepper flakes

2 tablespoons red wine vinegar

½ cup fresh parsley leaves

1 bunch of kale (1 pound), bottom 2 inches of stems removed

1 . Position a rack in the center of the oven and set the broiler to high.

2 . Evenly spread the chickpeas on a sheet pan and drizzle with up to 2 tablespoons olive oil. Season with salt and black pepper.

3 . On a second sheet pan, add the bell pepper halves, skin-side up, and the tomato. Broil the bell pepper and tomato until charred on one side, 4 to 5 minutes. Give the tomatoes a flip and let them broil until evenly charred, another 2 to 3 minutes. Transfer the bell pepper and tomato to a bowl and cover with either a lid or a plate to steam. Lower the oven temperature to 375°F.

4 . When the oven has reached 375°F, add the chickpeas and roast until they're light brown and crisp, 25 to 30 minutes.

5 . Meanwhile, peel the charred skins off the tomato and bell pepper and add them to a blender, along with the garlic, hazelnuts, chili powder, paprika, cinnamon, pepper flakes, vinegar, ¼ cup of the parsley, ¼ cup olive oil, and ½ teaspoon salt. Blend until smooth and season with salt. You want the sauce to be thick, like a drizzly nut butter.

6 . Tear the kale into big pieces, about 2 by 2 inches, and massage it with a drizzle of olive oil. When the chickpeas have 10 minutes left, scooch them to one side of the pan and add the kale to the other side, seasoning with a pinch of salt. Roast until the kale is crispy, about 10 more minutes.

7 . To serve, add a handful of kale leaves to each plate. Add ½ cup of chickpeas on top, then the romesco sauce. Top with the parsley.

HOTTIE TOMATO BEANS & CASHEW CREAM

Serves 2

This is a version of my favorite formula of cherry tomatoes, cooked down in olive oil and something spicy. The "something spicy" here is Aleppo pepper, which leans both fruity and subtly hot, which is good news for those of us with a lower spice tolerance. Another cooling element of this recipe is the cashew cream, which I like to swoop on a plate right before serving or dot on top of the beans in a fun design—if I'm feeling artistic. If you aren't in a cashew cream mood, this is also delicious made with ricotta or anything that can temper the punchiness of these peppery, sizzly beans.

Extra-virgin olive oil

1½ teaspoons Aleppo pepper flakes

2 teaspoons white sesame seeds

Freshly ground black pepper

1 garlic clove, grated

2 scallions, thinly sliced, white and green parts kept separate

1 pound (1 pint) cherry tomatoes, halved

Diamond Crystal kosher salt

1 (15-ounce) can white beans or chickpeas, drained and rinsed

¾ cup Cashew Cream (page 39)

Cooked rice or bread, for serving

1. Set a small pan over medium heat and add 3 tablespoons olive oil. Add the Aleppo pepper, sesame seeds, 1 teaspoon black pepper, the garlic, and scallion whites. Let this come to a soft simmer; when it sounds fizzy, give it a few swirls to turn it into a vibrant red oil, and cook for 2 minutes. Add the tomatoes and cook, stirring occasionally, for 8 to 10 minutes, watching the tomatoes break down into the sauce. Season with salt to taste.

2. Add the beans and swirl to coat. Cook for an additional minute or so to warm up the beans. Taste and season, as needed.

3. To serve, swipe a layer of cashew cream across the bottom of a plate or bowl and add the tomato-bean mixture on top. Garnish with the scallion greens and serve with rice or bread.

FAVA BEANS WITH PRESERVED LEMON RICOTTA

Serves 2

Fava beans come out in the spring and early summer, meaning they have always signaled warmth and sunshine in my brain. If you haven't prepared fresh fava beans before, they have two jackets: one is the fuzzy pod, and the other is a little shell around each bean that releases after a quick blanch. This salad is refreshingly cold, lemony, just the right level of creamy to be filling, and full of different bites of texture to the very end. If you're vegetarian, you can skip the anchovies in the bread crumbs, but if you aren't, enjoy the saltiness those flat-packed fillets give to this otherwise light, tangy, and herb-filled bowl.

¼ preserved lemon, homemade (see page 39) or store-bought

1 cup whole-milk ricotta

Diamond Crystal kosher salt

Freshly ground black pepper

35 fava bean pods (to yield about 2 cups fava beans; edamame is a great substitute)

Extra-virgin olive oil

3 flat anchovy fillets, packed in oil

¼ teaspoon red pepper flakes

½ cup Sourdough Bread Crumbs (page 46)

12 fresh basil leaves

10 fresh mint leaves

1 cup baby arugula

1 small watermelon radish, or 2 globe radishes, halved and thinly sliced

1½ tablespoons fresh lemon juice (about ½ lemon)

1 . Remove the pulp from the preserved lemon and finely chop it into a paste, thinly slice the rind and reserve it for later. In a small bowl, whisk the pulp into the ricotta, mixing quickly so the ricotta "fluffs" up. Season with salt and black pepper and set in the fridge while you prepare the rest of the salad.

2 . Shuck the fava beans from their pods by tearing off the stem end, pulling off the string down the center (or prying it open with your fingers), and pushing the beans out.

3 . Set a medium pot over high heat and bring 3 quarts of water to a boil. Salt the water liberally and add the fava beans. Let them boil for 1 to 2 minutes, while you prepare a bowl of ice water. Then use a slotted spoon to transfer the beans to the icy water. After a minute, you'll be able to pull the "jackets" off to release the smooth fava bean. Add all the beans to a large bowl.

4 . Drain the pot and set it back over medium heat. Add a drizzle of olive oil and the anchovies. Stirring constantly, watch the anchovies "melt" into the oil. Add the red pepper flakes and bread crumbs and stir to coat them in the anchovy oil. Toast, stirring occasionally, until the bread crumbs are golden, 3 to 4 minutes.

5 . Chiffonade-cut (see page 30) the basil and mint and add them to the fava beans, along with the sliced preserved lemon rind, arugula, and radish. Add the lemon juice and 1 tablespoon olive oil and mix. Season with salt and black pepper to taste.

6 . To serve, add a pile of the fluffy ricotta to each plate. Top with the fava bean salad and sprinkle everything generously with the anchovy bread crumbs.

LENTILS WITH STICKY SHALLOTS & DUKKAH

Serves 4

While I am on Team Any Bean, I am also vehemently on Team Only-Dried-Lentils, because I find canned lentils a little smushed and a little sad. These black lentils are versatile, perky, and capable of absorbing whatever flavors I throw at them; in this case, a sticky, vinegar-glazed shallot sauce. You begin the sauce on the stovetop to char the shallots and chilies; this then reduces them into melty oblivion in the oven. I use a stainless steel sauté pan (which is ovenproof up to something crazy like 800°F), so just make sure yours is, too. To contrast the caramelized, saucy lentils, I serve these with a swipe of cashew cream, crunchy dukkah, and a fistful of herbs. If you happen to have made the cream and dukkah earlier in the week as pantry staples, this comes together pretty quickly, but you can also use labneh or yogurt or store-bought dukkah if you have it.

Diamond Crystal kosher salt

1 cup dried black lentils

Extra-virgin olive oil

8 medium shallots, halved

2 Fresno peppers, seeded and halved

¼ cup red wine vinegar

¼ cup honey

Freshly ground black pepper

1 cup torn tender fresh herbs, such as cilantro, parsley, mint, basil

2 tablespoons fresh lime juice (about 1 limes)

FOR SERVING

1 cup Cashew Cream (page 39), yogurt, or labneh

¾ cup Pistachio Dukkah (page 42)

4 Broiled Yogurt Flatbreads (page 245; optional)

1 . Preheat the oven to 375°F. Set a medium pot over high heat and bring 3 quarts water to a boil. Add 1 tablespoon salt and the lentils and turn the heat down to simmer. Simmer until the lentils are cooked through but still have some bite to them, 13 to 15 minutes. Drain the lentils and set aside.

2 . While the lentils are simmering, set a large deep sauté pan over medium heat and add 3 tablespoons olive oil. Let the oil heat up for 1 to 2 minutes. Add the shallots cut-side down and cook, undisturbed, until they are deeply browned on both sides, 2 to 4 minutes per side. Push the shallots to the side of the pan and add the Fresno peppers skin-side down and cook for 2 minutes to char the skin, then flip them and turn off the heat.

3 . In a small bowl, whisk together the vinegar, honey, ¼ cup warm water, ¼ teaspoon salt, and a few cracks of black pepper. Pour this into the pan; it will reach halfway up the shallots.

4 . Transfer to the oven. Let it cook until the sauce is reduced by half and the shallots are a deep dark brown, 20 to 30 minutes.

5 . Remove the pan from the oven, add the lentils. and mix everything to coat. The lentils should be nicely glossy.

6 . In a small bowl, combine the herbs and lime juice. Season with a pinch of salt and toss. Add this to the lentils and give a quick mix.

7 . To serve, swipe the cashew cream into the side of a bowl. Scoop in the lentils and sprinkle with a generous amount of dukkah. Serve with flatbreads (if using).

GOCHUJANG BEANS WITH MELTY ESCAROLE & BLACK VINEGAR

Serves 4

Black vinegar, the sauce that is nearly mandatory alongside xiao long bao, is an ingredient I like to sneak into as many places as possible to add a note of acid and tang. Here, it's used to sharpen up some creamy butter beans in a glossy, sweet-spicy gochujang sauce. The recipe comes together fast, all in one pan, finishing with the melty escarole that clings to the beans almost like a dumpling wrapper—which, yes, *is a stretch*, until you scoop one up, wrap it around a bit of butter beans, and experience it for yourself. Serve this with steamed rice so the sauce can pool into that, too.

4 tablespoons salted butter

2 small shallots, thinly sliced

2 garlic cloves, finely grated

1 tablespoon finely grated fresh ginger

2 tablespoons gochujang

3 tablespoons rice vinegar

1 tablespoon soy sauce

1 tablespoon maple syrup

2 (15-ounce) cans butter beans, drained and rinsed

3 cups roughly torn escarole

¼ cup black vinegar, plus more to taste

1. Set a large pan over medium heat and add the butter. Let it melt, then cook, stirring occasionally, until the milk solids begin to brown, 3 to 4 minutes. Turn down the heat and add the shallots, stirring occasionally, until the shallots have softened and the butter is lightly golden brown, 2 to 4 minutes.

2. Meanwhile, in a large cup, whisk together the garlic, ginger, gochujang, vinegar, soy sauce, maple syrup, and 1 cup water.

3. Add the beans to the pan and give it a swirl to coat everything. Pour in the gochujang mixture, increase the heat to medium, and bring to a soft simmer. Let the sauce reduce by half, stirring occasionally, 5 to 6 minutes.

4. When the sauce becomes thick and glossy, add the escarole and let it wilt into the beans. This will take a matter of seconds.

5. To serve, portion into four bowls and dot each bowl with at least 1 tablespoon black vinegar, plus more as preferred.

CHARRED-TOMATO BEANS WITH TORN HERBS

Serves 4

If you come to my house during the summer, odds are you are going to get some rendition of this recipe, because in the three precious months that tomatoes are at the market, this charred-tomato dressing is always in my fridge. Although the dressing is perfect on its own, I add a pile of tender herb salad, because I'm probably buying herbs by the bushel at this point, and they make everything feel just a touch fresher. I encourage you to mix and match the color of the tomatoes; this will make the dish that much more beautiful.

Charred-Tomato Dressing (page 37), using assorted colors of tomatoes

2½ cups Basic_Beans (page 160), drained

15 large fresh basil leaves

½ cup fresh mint leaves

1 tablespoon fresh lemon juice (about ½ lemon)

Diamond Crystal kosher salt

½ loaf My Simplest Sourdough (page 235), preferably fresh but definitely warm

Freshly grated Parmesan cheese, for serving

1. In a large bowl, toss together the tomato dressing and the beans.

2. In a small bowl, tear in the basil and mint and top with the lemon juice. Season with salt and mix just enough so the herbs are combined but not smashed.

3. Scatter the herbs on top of the beans in the large bowl and do one big mix. Portion out into four individual bowls and serve with crusty sourdough and freshly grated Parmesan on top, following the Olive Garden rule: Stop when you're ready.

SIZZLED SAGE & OLIVE BEANS WITH RICOTTA SALATA

Serves 4

Calling all olive heads—this one's for you. My people-pleasing tendencies often steer me away from my hard-core, all-in obsession with olives, but with this quickly sizzled recipe, I caved. There's something about fried sage mixed with Kalamata olives that feels so delightfully *wrong* and *weird*, that I fixate on how well it works. The briny earthiness of the olives meets the crispy, aromatic sage, and when you add tangy ricotta salata (a harder, saltier cheese that you can find in most specialty cheese sections), it all makes sense. So bring on the weird, bring on the olives, bring on the cheese. Olive heads, it's time to party.

Extra-virgin olive oil

⅓ cup fresh sage leaves

½ cup Kalamata olives, finely chopped

4 garlic cloves, grated

½ cup fresh flat-leaf parsley, stems removed, leaves finely chopped

1 tablespoon Calabrian chili paste

2 teaspoons grated lemon zest (about 1 lemon)

2 (15-ounce) cans butter beans, drained and rinsed

3 tablespoons red wine vinegar

Diamond Crystal kosher salt

Freshly ground black pepper

4 ounces ricotta salata, cut into thick square slices

1 . Set a large pan over medium heat and add ⅓ cup olive oil. Let it heat up for 1 to 2 minutes, then add the sage leaves, letting them fry and sizzle until bright green and crisp, 1 to 2 minutes. Transfer them to a paper towel to drain.

2 . Add the olives and garlic to the pan and cook until the garlic is fragrant, 1 to 2 minutes. Add the parsley, chili paste, and lemon zest and cook for 1 to 2 minutes, stirring often. Add the beans and swirl to coat them in the sauce, then let them "sizzle" in the oil, undisturbed, for 2 to 3 minutes. Turn off the heat and finish with the vinegar. Taste and season with salt and black pepper.

3 . Crush in the sage leaves right before portioning into serving bowls. Top each bowl with a few slices of the ricotta salata.

SMASHED HONEYNUT BEANS WITH CRISPY SHROOMS

Serves 4

This is a gently spiced, very cozy cross between butternut squash soup and white bean soup, topped with my go-to oven-crisped mushrooms and Pecorino. I'm using honeynut squash, which was bred in 2008 (younger than most of us . . . probably?) and is the sweeter, more concentrated cousin (well, technically child) of the butternut squash. If you only have butternut on hand, that's totally fine; just use about one-third of a butternut for this recipe and you'll get a very similar result.

1 small honeynut squash
(8 ounces), seeded and halved

1 garlic bulb

Extra-virgin olive oil

½ pound oyster mushrooms

Diamond Crystal kosher salt

3 cups vegetable stock

1 teaspoon Calabrian chili
paste, plus more for garnish

2 (15-ounce) cans butter beans
or any white bean, drained and
rinsed

12 fresh sage leaves, chopped

1 tablespoon fresh thyme
leaves, chopped

1 tablespoon fresh rosemary,
chopped

Freshly ground black pepper

2 ounces (about ⅔ cup) freshly
grated Parmesan cheese,
for serving

1. Equally stagger two racks in the oven and preheat it to 400°F. Line a sheet pan with parchment paper.

2. Place the squash halves cut-sides down on the lined sheet pan. Cut off the top off of the garlic bulb to expose the cloves. Drizzle the garlic with 1 tablespoon olive oil and wrap in aluminum foil. Roast both on the bottom rack of the oven until softened, 25 to 30 minutes—setting a timer for 12 minutes; that's when you'll add the mushrooms.

3. While the squash is roasting, tear the mushrooms into thin strips. Add them to another sheet pan. Drizzle with 1 tablespoon olive oil and season with salt.

4. Slide the sheet pan of mushrooms onto the top rack of the oven and roast until the mushrooms are dark brown and extremely crispy, 15 to 18 minutes.

5. Let the squash cool, then remove the skin and add the squash to a blender along with the vegetable stock. Squeeze in the roasted garlic cloves, add the chili paste and ¼ teaspoon of salt, and blend until smooth.

6. Set a large Dutch oven over medium heat and add 2 tablespoons olive oil to the pan. Add the beans and swirl in the oil. Add the sage, thyme, and rosemary and cook for another minute.

7. Pour in the honeynut broth and bring to a gentle simmer. While the broth is simmering, use a spatula or a spoon to gently smash the beans. You want almost no pieces still whole, making the soup a chunky, creamy texture. Simmer for 5 to 8 minutes, until the soup has thickened, smashing as you go. Taste and season with salt and black pepper.

8. To serve, portion into four bowls and top each with the crispy mushrooms and a generous grating of cheese. Dot with chili paste to taste.

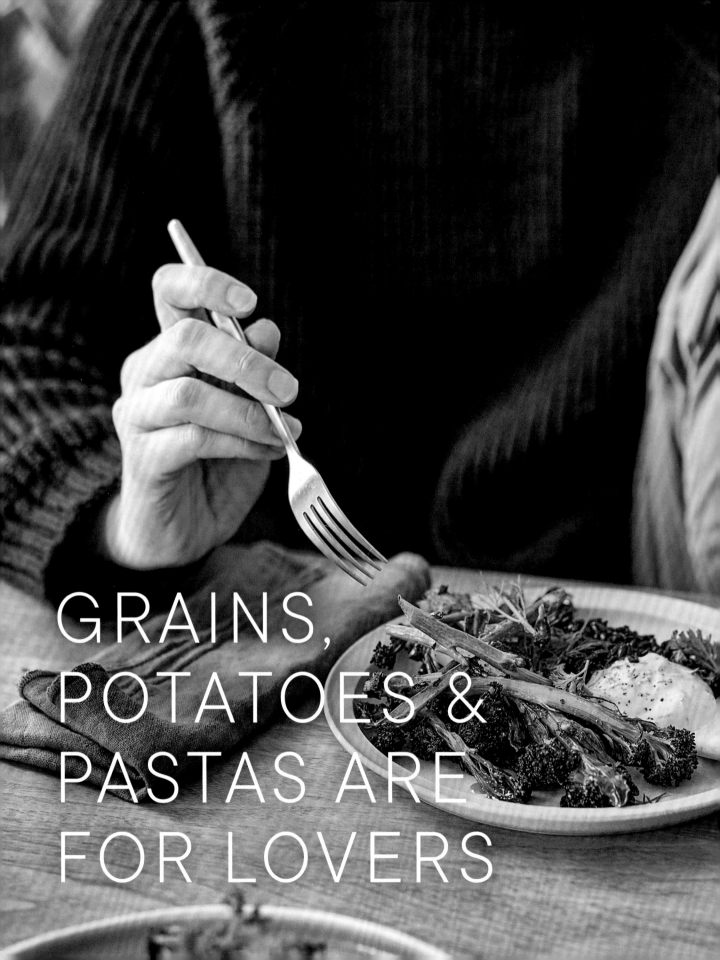

GRAINS,
POTATOES &
PASTAS ARE
FOR LOVERS

YOU SHOULDN'T PICK A FAVORITE FOOD GROUP, because variety is the spice of life. But I do. I just do. Grains, potatoes, and pastas—basically anything that could have fit in the bottom of a 1990s food pyramid, I've loved.

And the argument about what a grain, pasta, or starchy thing can and cannot do has always been interesting to me. Like potatoes: Must be a side. Pasta: A definite meal. Rice? Side. Fried rice? Meal, depending on who you ask. But no matter if it's a side, a meal, or leftovers eaten out of my fridge, these foods give me a hit of comfort on my plate, and they have a special way of tying everything together.

Here, I try to bridge the gaps of what these grain-y things can be. We have spice-crusted potatoes, a bright lemon risotto, cast-iron crispy rice, and vegetable-packed orzo with a shattering, cheesy top. Most of these dishes are meant to be a full meal (the black rice and tonnato situation on page 191 will keep you full for days), whereas others are up for interpretation, like the comfort that only a bowl of Brown Butter Tahini on Any Noodle (page 199) can provide; which is essentially my adult version of buttered noodles.

The point of this chapter is not to stress over what part of the meal these make up but to make sure they're cooked with enough flavor to stand on their own. It's my love letter to every grain, pasta, or potato I've ever met, because they deserve that, right?

ROASTED POTATOES WITH OLIVE & RED ONION DRESSING

Serves 4

There's a vendor at my farmers' market who really thrives in the hot peppers and potatoes department. During the year, you can find them selling at minimum ten kinds of potatoes and at season's peak in late summer/early fall, around twenty. Each with a cute little label, like "Adirondack Blues—great for roasting!" (PS: They *are* great for roasting and equally good for niçoise salads, just FYI.) And I feel lucky to live in a time where all the research on how to make the perfect roasted potato has already been done for me, leaving me to make a punchy, lemony dressing that can stand up to the potato's craggily edges. You don't need Adirondack Blues for this, just any potato that is starchy enough to crisp up to its full potato potential: Think the classics, like Yukon Gold, russet, or fingerling.

1½ pounds good roasting potatoes

½ teaspoon baking soda

Diamond Crystal kosher salt

Extra-virgin olive oil

½ small red onion, thinly sliced

3 tablespoons fresh lemon juice (about 1 lemon), plus more to taste

1 teaspoon Aleppo pepper flakes

2 ounces pitted green olives, such as Castelvetrano, finely chopped (about ⅓ cup)

½ cup torn tender fresh herbs, such as parsley, mint, dill

1 . Position a rack in the center of the oven and preheat it to 450°F.

2 . Cut the potatoes into 1½-inch chunks.

3 . Set a large pot over high heat and bring 2 quarts water to a boil. Add the baking soda and 2 tablespoons salt. Add the potatoes and boil until fork-tender, 12 to 15 minutes.

4 . Transfer the potatoes to a sheet pan, add 3 tablespoons olive oil, and toss to coat. Season with ¼ teaspoon salt. Roast until deeply golden and crispy on the edges, 20 to 25 minutes.

5 . While the potatoes are roasting, in a small bowl, combine the onion and lemon juice. Let this sit for 5 minutes. Add the Aleppo pepper, a big pinch of salt, the olives, and herbs. Mix together and add more salt and lemon juice as needed.

6 . When the potatoes are out of the oven, add them to a serving platter and scatter the dressing all over.

7 . When eating, scoop the dressing up with the potatoes for a hit in each bite.

CRUSTED SWEET POTATOES & PEPITAS

Serves 4

As someone with a notorious sweet-meets-savory tooth, sweet potatoes have a special place in my heart. Their only flaw is *really bad* marketing. There's a rumor that you can make sweet potatoes crispy, which—I hate to divulge—is a lie. I can hear the counterarguments swirling as I write this, but in my testing, no amount of ice-bath soaking, freezing, frying, or cornstarch can achieve the same crisp that you get with their standard potato counterparts—unless it is a sweet potato waffle fry, which, I've determined, is either cheating and/or magic. But why try to make something be what it's not? A sweet potato's best quality is its soft, creamy texture, so my answer is to add the crunch directly on top. Here the potatoes are torn, dressed in a spicy, cinnamon-y oil, and piled with craggily pumpkin seed bread crumbs. The heat of the oil is up to you; it gets spicier the longer you let it sit before straining—2 minutes gets it plenty spicy for me.

4 small sweet potatoes
(6 ounces each)

Extra-virgin olive oil

1 teaspoon red pepper flakes

½ teaspoon ground cinnamon

½ teaspoon smoked paprika

2 teaspoons red wine vinegar

2 tablespoons honey

Diamond Crystal kosher salt

2 tablespoons pumpkin seeds,
coarsely chopped

Freshly ground black pepper

¼ cup Sourdough Bread
Crumbs (page 46)

1. Position a rack in the center of the oven and preheat it to 425°F.

2. Pierce the sweet potatoes with a fork, then wrap each in aluminum foil and roast until soft and fork-tender, 40 to 45 minutes. Keep them wrapped but set them aside to cool. This makes them extra soft.

3. Set a small pan over medium heat and combine ¼ cup olive oil and the pepper flakes. Bring to a simmer, then add the cinnamon and paprika, swirl together, and immediately turn off the heat. Pour through a fine-mesh sieve into a heatproof bowl to strain out the pepper flakes. Whisk in the vinegar, honey, and a few pinches of salt.

4. Wipe out any leftover pepper flakes from the pan and add the pumpkin seeds. Set the pan back over medium heat and toast, stirring occasionally, until they are a shade darker and fragrant, 3 to 4 minutes. Add ¼ teaspoon black pepper and the bread crumbs, drizzle with olive oil, and cook until the bread crumbs are golden, another 5 minutes. Remove from the heat and season with salt.

5. Tear (yes, tear!—we want the imperfect edges) the potatoes into big, rough chunks. Add these to a bowl and drizzle with the spicy oil, reserving a few teaspoons. Mix a few times to coat, then transfer to a serving dish. Sprinkle generously with the bread crumbs and spoon the reserved spicy oil over the top. A few more cracks of black pepper will live happily here.

CRISPY RICE IN SUNGOLD-MISO BROTH

Serves 2 as a meal or 4 as a side

I used to live above a sushi and noodles restaurant (aptly named Sushi & Noodles), whose owner my fiancé and I referred to as Mom. The nickname started because whenever one of us was sick, the other would go downstairs and get a cup of miso soup and a cup of white rice for $3 that, I swear, had healing power. This is an homage to that combo, with sweet Sungold tomatoes thrown into the mix for brightness (and vitamin C!) and islands of crispy rice (a good use for leftover take-out rice, if you have any). It's healing on its own or serve it on a platter alongside Black Garlic Sea Bass (page 214) or Crispy Tofu (page 207), to make your sick-day soup a full meal.

1 cup short-grain white rice

2 scallions

Extra-virgin olive oil

1 pound (1 pint) Sungold tomatoes, halved

1 tablespoon white miso paste

½ cup hot water

1 teaspoon grated fresh ginger

2 tablespoons avocado oil

1 . Cook the rice according to the package directions.

2 . Meanwhile, slice the scallions lengthwise into long, thin strips and, if you'd like, add them to an ice bath to get them extra curled up and crisp.

3 . Set a small pan over medium heat and add 1 tablespoon olive oil. Add the tomatoes and let them cook, shaking the pan occasionally until they begin to collapse, 5 to 6 minutes.

4 . While the tomatoes are cooking, in a small bowl, whisk the miso paste into the hot water, letting it dissolve fully.

5 . Add the miso mixture and ginger to the tomatoes. Let this come to a simmer and cook to reduce by half, 9 to 12 minutes. Transfer to a serving bowl.

6 . Wipe out the pan and add the avocado oil. Set the pan back over medium heat, add the rice, and press down into a flat layer with a spatula. Cook for 5 to 6 minutes, undisturbed, until the bottom of the rice is golden and crispy. Then break it into a few big pieces; they don't have to be perfect. Flip each piece out of the pan onto the tomatoes.

7 . Top with the scallions and use a spoon to break the crispy rice to get down to the juicy, tomatoey broth below.

A BIT ON COOKING GRAINS

In this chapter, I have a few recipes, where I say "Cook X according to the package directions." This is because there are huge variations in cooking times and water ratios across different grains, types of rice, and brands of rice cooker . . . and frankly, I don't want to lead you astray. I have a powerhouse rice cooker that handles most grains well with a 2:1 ratio of water to grain, but saying "use the rice cooker I bought in 2016," probably isn't an incredibly helpful instruction.

Most rice and grain packages tend to have the most helpful instructions, but when in doubt, I use the "pasta" method—cooking the grains in salted boiling water and testing around the 10- to 20-minute mark. Depending on the package's suggested cooking time or a quick internet search, you can get a feel for how quickly your grains will be done.

BLACK RICE, BLISTERED GREENS & HERBY TONNATO

Serves 4

This dish is like a pescatarian take on one-pot chicken, nestled in rice. It's deeply comforting, with a wonderful nuttiness from the black rice and crispy-edged broccolini on top—though any hearty green will work. I've done Lacinato kale, Swiss chard, and mustard greens (sliced into long ribbons). Topping everything with creamy tonnato gives you that hit of protein—just in sauce form—so I count this rice-centric pan as a perfect dinner.

Extra-virgin olive oil

½ small sweet onion, diced

Diamond Crystal kosher salt

1 cup black rice

¼ cup dry unoaked white wine

2½ cups vegetable stock

8 ounces broccolini

¼ cup fresh dill, stems removed, plus more for garnish

1 cup Tonnato (page 36)

1 tablespoon curly parsley leaves, for garnish (optional)

Freshly ground black pepper

1 tablespoon Calabrian chili oil or a hot sauce such as Frank's RedHot

Lemon wedges, for squeezing

1. Set a large, deep ovenproof sauté pan over medium heat and add 2 tablespoons olive oil. Add the onion and cook, stirring occasionally, until soft, 6 to 7 minutes. Season with a pinch of salt. Add the rice, mix to coat it in the oil and onion, and toast until it smells nutty and delicious, 30 to 60 seconds. Pour in the wine and let it reduce for 2 to 3 minutes. Season with ½ teaspoon salt, add the stock, and bring to a simmer. Cover the pan and let simmer until the majority of the liquid is gone, 25 to 30 minutes.

2. Meanwhile, position a rack in the center of the oven and preheat it to 425°F.

3. Cut the broccolini into long thin strips, slicing through the stem. Add the strips to a bowl and toss with 1 tablespoon olive oil and a pinch of salt.

4. When the rice has been simmering for 25 to 30 minutes, leaving a flat surface of rice, nestle the broccolini on top of the rice and move to the oven. Bake, uncovered, until the broccolini is browned on top and the rice is cooked throughout, 20 to 22 minutes.

5. While the rice finishes in the oven, finely chop the dill and stir it into the tonnato.

6. To serve, spoon the tonnato over the rice and broccolini. Garnish with some dill and the parsley (if using) and a few cracks of black pepper. Dot with the chili oil. Serve with lemon wedges for squeezing over the broccolini.

WHOLE LEMON-SAFFRON COUSCOUS

Serves 4

When I was first taught to make saffron rice, the rice was poured over sautéed onion and simmered in stock, using crushed saffron threads that had been bloomed in ice, never hot water. (A Persian friend told me this was integral to preserving its flavor and aroma and never lets me forget it.) And without fail, whenever I use saffron, this simple, colorful ingredient proves why it's one of the most expensive spices in the world. It's musky but sweet, richly aromatic, and distinctly itself. This couscous is a twist on saffron rice, where the onion cooks down with a whole lemon that caramelizes into a sticky-sharp flavor, finishing the couscous in a lemon "broth" of sorts. Everything mellows alongside the saffron, making a fluffy side dish so balanced that I want to scoop up more, and more . . . and more.

¼ teaspoon high-quality saffron threads

2 ice cubes (up to 60ml of water)

Extra-virgin olive oil

1 lemon, very thinly sliced, seeds removed

1 medium yellow onion, thinly sliced

Diamond Crystal kosher salt

2 Thai red chilies, thinly sliced

3 garlic cloves, thinly sliced

1 cup Moroccan couscous

1. Use a mortar and pestle to crush the saffron threads. Bloom the saffron by sprinkling the saffron powder over 2 ice cubes. Set this aside and allow the ice cubes to melt while you prepare the rest of the recipe.

2. Set a large, deep sauté pan with a fitted lid over medium heat and add 6 tablespoons olive oil. Add the lemon, onion, and a few generous pinches of salt. Cook, stirring occasionally, until the onion and lemon are softened, 17 to 20 minutes. Pick out any stray lemon seeds as you go.

3. Add the chilies and garlic to the pan and cook until the lemon begins to caramelize and darken, 5 to 10 minutes. Pour in the couscous and give one big mix to ease it into the onion and lemon. Drizzle the saffron water evenly over top. Pour in 1 cup of water and stir to combine. Let this come to a simmer (it should take seconds), then turn off the heat and cover. Let this stand on the stove for 5 minutes. Uncover and fluff the couscous, season with a few large pinches of salt, and mix again.

SHATTER TOP CAULIFLOWER ORZO

Serves 4

Ever since people started turning cauliflower into rice, I wanted to make a recipe that was cauliflower *with* rice as my cheeky little aside to the trend. My vision was not just flecks of cauliflower and rice, though, I wanted a full-blown cheesy, peppery cauliflower cream. Think: Alfredo-adjacent but still very much a veg. And it turns out, after a few cauliflowers and errors, the pasta version knocked the rice version out of the running. The "shatter top" element comes from baking a quick frico, a fancy term for what is essentially a large cheese-chip, but if you don't want to turn on your oven, it's equally good with a mountain of Parmesan.

Extra-virgin olive oil

4 garlic cloves, smashed then peeled

3 cups cauliflower florets (½ a large head)

Diamond Crystal kosher salt

Freshly ground black pepper

⅛ teaspoon red pepper flakes

4 ounces Parmesan cheese, freshly grated (about 1⅓ cups)

½ preserved lemon, homemade (see page 39) or store-bought, plus 1 tablespoon of brine

4 cups vegetable stock

1 pound orzo

1. Position a rack in the top of the oven and preheat it to 400°F. Line a sheet pan with parchment paper.

2. Set a large pot over medium heat and add 3 tablespoons olive oil. Add the garlic and let it sizzle for a minute or so. Add the cauliflower and cook, stirring occasionally, until the cauliflower is fully soft, 7 to 9 minutes. Season with a large pinch of salt, a few cracks of black pepper, and the pepper flakes.

3. Transfer the cauliflower and garlic to a blender. Add ½ cup of Parmesan to the blender along with the lemon, brine, and 1 cup of the vegetable broth. Blend until very smooth (this takes me 2 to 3 minutes of blending). Taste and season, as preferred, but I find the cheese and lemon get it plenty salty.

4. In the same pot, bring the remaining 3 cups of vegetable broth to a boil and add the orzo. Boil until most of the broth has been absorbed into the orzo, 6 to 8 minutes. Pour in the cauliflower cream, turn off the heat, and stir to combine. If needed to keep everything smooth, add a few splashes of hot water.

5. Grate the remaining Parmesan and spread it into four large rounds on the lined sheet pan, making each round the same size as the shoulder of the dishes you plan to serve the orzo in. Bake until you have lightly golden and crisp fricos, 6 to 7 minutes.

6. To serve, portion the orzo into four bowls. Gently place the frico on top and use a spoon to, well, shatter!

PROSECCO-KALE RISOTTO

Serves 4

I like to pretend risotto was built on the premise that cooking and drinking together is one of life's most enjoyable activities. If I'm going to stand at a stove for over 60 minutes for a leisure activity (and I promise, making risotto *is* a leisure activity!), I'd like a drink.

This risotto is wonderfully light and simple, and I'm not sure if that's due to the Prosecco or to how much fun I have while cooking it. A good rule of thumb is to choose a crisp, bubbly wine that's cheap enough to cook with but good enough to drink. My next rule is to have a few friends to share it with, because while the risotto process is slow, a healthy amount of gossip speeds it up tenfold.

Diamond Crystal kosher salt

Extra-virgin olive oil

½ small white onion, diced

1 cup risotto rice, such as Arborio

½ cup Prosecco or dry unoaked white wine

3 tablespoons salted butter

2 cups kale, stems removed, torn

3 tablespoons fresh lemon juice (about 1 lemon)

1 ounce (about ½ cup) Parmesan cheese, freshly grated

Freshly ground black pepper

1 . Set a large pot over high heat and bring at least 2 quarts water to a low simmer. Season it with 1 tablespoon salt.

2 . At the same time, set a deep sauté pan over medium heat and add ¼ cup olive oil. Add the onion, season with a few pinches of salt, and cook, stirring occasionally, until the onion is soft, 5 to 7 minutes. Add a splash of water and continue to cook, until the onion is completely soft and almost melty, another 4 to 5 minutes.

3 . Add the rice to the onion and stir quickly to make sure it is completely coated in the onion and oil. Cook until you see the sides of the rice turn clear, about another 5 minutes. This means the grain has taken on some of the oil, and it's time to add the Prosecco. Let the Prosecco simmer to cook off the alcohol, 2 to 3 minutes.

4 . Scoop a large ladle of the simmering water, around ¾ cup, into the risotto and stir constantly until the water is absorbed. For the next 20 to 25 minutes, keep repeating in 3-minute intervals, until the risotto becomes thick, creamy, and soft. This is also the time to pour a glass of wine, have a chat with your cooking partners, tear up your kale . . . you get it.

5 . Test the rice after 20 minutes and if the grains are soft with no tough bite to them, they're finished. It might need up to 30 to 35 minutes, though, so take your time.

6 . Once the rice has reached a soft texture, turn both burners off but leave the pan of rice on the stovetop. Stir the butter into the risotto to combine. Add the kale and gently stir to let the heat from the risotto wilt the greens. Squeeze in the lemon juice and season with salt to taste.

7 . Stir in half the Parmesan here and save the other half for topping. If you need to, add another splash of water from the big pot to thin things out.

8 . Serve in four big bowls topped with the remaining Parmesan and some black pepper.

BROWN BUTTER TAHINI ON ANY NOODLE

Serves 4

This recipe is essentially buttered noodles for adults (even though buttered noodles are also for adults but . . . you get what I mean). And if I'm going to flex how easy they are, they're the same commitment as Kraft macaroni and cheese, give or take a noodle. Since tahini occasionally stiffens up if it sits too long, you'll need to include a generous scoop (or two) of pasta water to keep things smooth and saucy. And while it's always tempting to skip a garnish, a few sprigs of mint beautifully break up the richness of the nutty sauce.

Diamond Crystal kosher salt

8 ounces pasta, such as pappardelle, cascatelli, reginetti, or your favorite pasta shape

4 tablespoons salted butter

1 teaspoon grated lemon zest (about ½ lemon)

½ teaspoon Aleppo pepper flakes, plus more for garnish

¼ cup tahini

1 tablespoon fresh lemon juice (about ½ lemon)

Torn fresh mint leaves, for garnish

Freshly ground black pepper

1. Set a large pot of water next to a large deep sauté pan on your stovetop—you'll be working with both of these simultaneously.

2. Bring the pot of water to a boil and add 2 teaspoons salt. Add the pasta to the boiling water and cook until al dente, according to package directions.

3. Set the sauté pan over medium heat and add the butter. When the butter has melted and begins to brown slightly, around the 3- to 4-minute mark, add the lemon zest and Aleppo pepper and turn the heat to medium-low.

4. When the pasta is nearly ready, pour the tahini into the butter mixture and stir for a few seconds to combine. As soon as the pasta is ready, use a slotted spoon to transfer the pasta directly into the pan. Add ½ cup pasta water to the pan and mix quickly to combine. Add the lemon juice and continue to stir. Taste and season with salt. Mix, continuing to add splashes of pasta water, until you get a smooth, glossy, tahini butter sauce.

5. Scoop the pasta onto a plate and garnish with the mint, black pepper, and a sprinkle of Aleppo pepper.

SPAETZLE NIGHT

It is common knowledge that my kitchen is small, but my heart is big, meaning I am ill-equipped to host dinners, but I am definitely going to try. In 2021, I decided spaetzle would be my entertaining "thing," inviting friends for what would inevitably turn into spaetzle night. Spaetzle is fresh pasta-adjacent but not fresh pasta, and I like how it loosely ties to my German roots (roots I know nothing about, to be fair). I also like that it can feed enough people for a small dinner but not a big one. Intimate, because my tiny-dumpling-noodles couldn't handle the pressure of a crowd.

Spaetzle is a wet batter, think pancake batter consistency, and when you pour it into a ricer, it drops into little dumplings, almost like gnocchi you don't need to roll out. I make the spaetzle right before we eat, mostly because half the promise of spaetzle night is dinner and a show, so everyone takes their turn at dripping the batter into the simmer pot. We've had tomato confit spaetzle nights, goat cheese and beet spaetzle nights (it did look like a horror movie, but it was good!), garlic scape and basil spaetzle

nights, and the great gluten-free spaetzle night debacle of 2022, which we don't talk about.

The nice part about spaetzle nights is they aren't dinner parties per se—they're just dinner. Everything is served from the Dutch oven it was cooked in, bowls are usually mismatched, and any drinks are typically guest-provided, meaning the food and wine pairing is a complete toss-up. The crowd is small enough that the stakes are low, meaning the fun levels are high.

I chose spaetzle to be my hosting "thing," because I liked the sound of it, but the more I've made it, the more I've realized it's a food that very much feels like me: cozy, approachable, low-maintenance, and best with a small group.

And, yes, I vote for your trying to make spaetzle at least once, so you can see what I mean, but I'm also an advocate for finding your own hosting "thing." Be it spaetzle or something else, a small dinner tradition carries more weight than just the food.

SQUASH & DILL SPAETZLE

Serves 4

Spaetzle, a German dumpling-noodle hybrid, is a simple dish and easy to master once you get the hang of it, but it takes a bit of time to catch on to the technique. The irony is, when you're in the actual act of making spaetzle, you have only a few minutes to boil it to a perfectly light, bouncy al dente, so the technique part happens quickly. You will need a ricer or a slotted spoon to make this, but if this is your first attempt at spaetzle, don't worry; this recipe is worth your time. Sweet and hearty butternut squash cook down into tender fall-apart pieces that mix with a touch of nutmeg and pepper to make it feel as cozy as possible. And there is no sense of accomplishment like spaetzle accomplishment—just trust me.

   This spaetzle made its first appearance on February 2, 2023, and it has appeared at multiple cold-weather spaetzle nights since. It's meant for four hungry people, or six not-as-hungry people but can be scaled up or down as you need. My one note is that it tastes best served straight from the pot, and I have people who will back me up on that.

Extra-virgin olive oil

1 tablespoon salted butter

1 small yellow onion,
thinly sliced

Diamond Crystal kosher salt

4 garlic cloves, grated

1 small butternut squash
(1½ pounds), peeled and cut
into 1-inch cubes

¼ teaspoon red pepper flakes

¼ teaspoon ground nutmeg

2 large eggs

1 cup (140g) all-purpose flour

¾ cup vegetable or chicken
stock

Freshly ground black pepper

1 cup fresh dill, stems removed,
coarsely chopped

1. Set a large Dutch oven over medium heat and add 6 tablespoons olive oil and the butter. Add the onion and cook, stirring occasionally, until soft, 5 to 6 minutes. Season with a pinch of salt.

2. Add the garlic, squash, pepper flakes, and nutmeg and stir to coat in the fat. Season with another generous pinch of salt. Cover but leave the lid cracked. Cook, stirring every 5 minutes or so, for 20 minutes. In the last 5 minutes, gently break up the squash, mashing some pieces and leaving some whole.

3. Meanwhile, in a large bowl, whisk the eggs. Add the flour, ½ teaspoon salt, and 6 tablespoons cool water. Whisk together to make the spaetzle batter. Let this sit and thicken for 10 minutes.

4. When the squash is nice and soft, add the stock and simmer for another 5 minutes, stirring occasionally. Turn off the heat but leave the Dutch oven on the burner.

5. Set a large pot of water next to the Dutch oven and bring it to a simmer. Add 1 teaspoon salt. Using a ricer (with the 5mm disk attached) and a spatula, pour the spaetzle batter into the ricer in three rounds. Softly press the spaetzle batter out of the ricer with the spatula, watching it drop little dumpling pieces into the simmering water. Cook each round of spaetzle

NOTE: I don't eat poultry, but this recipe also works well with chicken stock, which my meatier friends have told me is a game changer.

until they all float, 3 to 4 minutes. Use a slotted spoon or spider to skim the spaetzle out of the water and transfer directly to the Dutch oven.

6 . Once all the spaetzle are in with the squash, add ¼ cup of the cooking water and stir to combine. It should be thick and almost creamy, with large pieces of butternut squash throughout. Taste and season with salt and black pepper, as needed.

7 . To finish, add the dill to the Dutch oven and swirl it in. Serve warm.

MY
KIND OF
PROTEINS

I'M A PESCATARIAN—BUT I TRY TO KEEP THAT ON THE DL. Not because I'm embarrassed, but because I've found when I don't mention it, people don't usually notice. That is, of course, before I was tasked with lining up a whole list of my favorite proteins, so now it felt like I had some explaining to do.

One thing I want to clear up is that plant-based cooking requires just as much technique as preparing meat. (It bothers me that it's sometimes viewed as simpler and less skillful. Untrue!) Cooking vegetarian proteins is cooking, with the same amount of prep, attention, and care. But similar to when you learned to first roast a chicken to its peak-juicy potential, here I hope to show you how to press tofu to its max crispiness, how to simmer tempeh to alleviate some of its funk, and how to coax fiery flavor into a faux sausage (delicious; see page 209).

And if you're like me, with a heavy respect for plant-based cooking but a side that is a solid fish fiend, you'll see that fish fits into "my kind" of proteins, too. There are simple weeknight dishes (Boyfriend Salmon, page 217, is something to make on repeat) all the way to the Littleneck Clams with Preserved Lemon Butter (page 226) that carry nearly every dinner party I throw. The thing I promise is that each protein, from plant to ocean, showcases a different strategy for maximizing flavor and making your dinner as vibrant as can be. These are my kinds of protein, but I hope they become yours, too.

SLICEABLE BALSAMIC TOFU

Serves 4

I call this my sandwich tofu; it acts as my deli meat and the closest thing I can get to a bodega Boar's Head counter, so I cherish it. The key to this preparation is two types of moisture release: the first is when you press the tofu, and the second is when you bake it low and slow. Unlike meat, toughening up tofu can be a good thing, leaving a dense, almost juicy consistency that's easy to thinly slice. The slices store well in the fridge for up to a week, so late-night sandwiches are taken care of.

1 (16-ounce) block extra-firm tofu

¼ cup balsamic vinegar

¼ cup Worcestershire sauce

¼ cup soy sauce

2 tablespoons dark brown sugar

3 garlic cloves, grated

1 teaspoon grated fresh ginger

Freshly ground black pepper

1. Cut the tofu crosswise into five even rectangular pieces and press using the method opposite.

2. In a small saucepan, combine the vinegar, Worcestershire sauce, soy sauce, brown sugar, garlic, ginger, and ¼ teaspoon pepper. Bring to a soft simmer, and cook for 5 to 6 minutes, stirring occasionally. The sauce won't fully reduce, but it will still be pretty thin.

3. Place the pressed tofu either in a large plastic bag or a storage container and pour the marinade over the tofu. Seal and let it sit in your fridge for 3 hours or up to 1 day. The longer it sits, the more the marinade it will absorb. If the marinade doesn't completely cover the tofu, flip it about halfway through the marinating time.

4. When you're ready to bake, preheat the oven to 375°F. Line a sheet pan with parchment paper.

5. Take the tofu out of the marinade but reserve the marinade. Arrange the tofu on the lined sheet pan and bake until it's firm and sliceable, 45 to 50 minutes. To use it throughout the week, store it in the fridge in an airtight container with ¼ cup of the leftover marinade. It will keep for slicing and serving for 1 week.

CRISPY TOFU, WITH JUST TOFU

Serves 4

This recipe feels almost too boring to belong here, but it made the list because of its versatility and the fact that it sees my kitchen at least once a week. The technique is simple: Press out any excess moisture from the tofu and sear it until a beautifully golden and crisp crust forms. It takes a bit of time, but its utility is the reward for your patience. It's a blank-canvas tofu, so if you are looking for protein in a salad, curry, or soup, this recipe belongs in your back pocket.

If you're looking for some ideas of what to eat with this tofu, try Crispy Rice in Sungold-Miso Broth (page 188), Baked Kale Salad with Chili Quinoa (page 113), Basil Cucumbers with Slightly Sweet Peanuts (page 118), or Cauliflower with Coconut Dressing & Fresno Almonds (page 147).

1 (16-ounce) block extra-firm tofu

Diamond Crystal kosher salt

Avocado oil, or any neutral oil with a high smoke point, such as canola, vegetable, grapeseed, or sunflower

1 . Cut the block of tofu crosswise into five even rectangles, each about 1 inch thick. Slice each rectangle in half to make two squares, then slice the squares diagonally to make tiny tofu triangles. (You can also cut the tofu however you prefer; it's up to you!)

2 . Press the tofu (see below). When you uncover the tofu, season both sides of the pieces with a pinch of salt.

3 . Set a large sauté pan over medium heat and add the avocado oil until it just coats the entire base of the pan. Heat the oil until it gets to 325°F. Working in batches, add the tofu and cook until the tofu is a deep brown and is crisp on both sides, 3 to 4 minutes per side. Patience is key—you'll be surprised at the difference in color and crispness a minute or two makes. Transfer the tofu to a dry paper towel to drain and then use it however you'd like.

HOW I PRESS TOFU

My tofu recipes may differ, but my pressing method stays the same.

First, drain and lightly press out any moisture from the tofu with a few paper towels. Slice the tofu into the preferred size for the recipe.

Get two sheet pans of the same size and line one with paper towels or a lint-free dish towel. Place all the pieces on the towel-lined sheet pan and add another layer of towels on top. Place the second sheet pan on top and weight it down with 1 or 2 heavy books (this book is happy to be of service for that!). Press for at least 15 minutes, but 30 is best.

'NDUJA, BUT NOT

Makes 1½ cups

My biggest jealousy in this life is 'nduja—the Italian sausage spread that graces pasta, pizzas, toasts, and somehow everything I want to order at an Italian restaurant, precisely when I want to order it. 'Nduja is decidedly meaty, and I am decidedly meat-less, so my only solution was to create a vegetarian 'nduja of my own, with a hit of tomato paste for acid, chili paste for heat, and a splash of smoke to mimic the peppery sausage's aroma. It was a bit of a mad science project, but after serving it to my sausage-inclined friends, it got a rating as close to the real thing. Eat it on toast, with ricotta bowls, stirred into your fresh pasta, or thrown into salads and grain bowls.

Extra-virgin olive oil

1 teaspoon fennel seeds

3 tablespoons tomato paste

3 garlic cloves, grated

1½ teaspoons Calabrian chili paste

1 teaspoon red miso paste

1 teaspoon liquid smoke

One half (16-ounce) block of firm or extra-firm tofu

Diamond Crystal kosher salt

Freshly ground black pepper

1. Set a large pan over medium heat and add 2 tablespoons olive oil and the fennel seeds. Toast the fennel seeds until fragrant, about 1 minute.

2. In a small bowl, mix together the tomato paste, garlic, chili paste, miso, and liquid smoke. Add this to the pan and cook until the mixture is a shade darker, 3 to 5 minutes.

3. Use a fork to break up the tofu into big crumbs. Add the tofu to the pan and stir to combine, cooking another 2 to 3 minutes to cook off any excess moisture.

4. Season with salt and black pepper and turn off the heat. From here, you can serve or store in the fridge for up to 1 week.

CREAMY TEMPEH WITH HERB SALAD & FLUFFY FLATBREADS

Serves 2

Tempeh often gets overlooked for other plant-based proteins because of its distinctive "funk." I have never minded the funk, seeing as I'm a soybean and fermentation enthusiast, so I let tempeh be tempeh—surrounding it with a spice-driven creamy coconut sauce and enough herbs to make every bite feel half-curry, half-salad. The goal is to pan-fry the tempeh to the perfect crisp, then focus on building up the ingredients around it—making sure that everything can match its valuable, irreplaceable funk.

1 (8-ounce) block tempeh

2 tablespoons neutral oil, such as avocado or canola

½ medium red onion, thinly sliced

Diamond Crystal kosher salt

2 garlic cloves, grated

1 tablespoon grated fresh ginger

2 teaspoons ground turmeric

1 teaspoon ground coriander

1 teaspoon ground cumin

¼ teaspoon red pepper flakes

¼ preserved lemon, homemade (see page 39) or store-bought, plus 2 teaspoons brine

1 (13.5-ounce) can full-fat coconut milk

Freshly ground black pepper

½ cup tender fresh herbs, such as parsley, mint, cilantro, coarsely chopped

2 Broiled Yogurt Flatbreads (page 245) or any store-bought flatbreads

1 . Cube the tempeh into chunks. (I like to make them about the size of a garlic clove to keep the size consistent across all pieces.)

2 . Set a large pan over medium heat and add the neutral oil. Add the tempeh and pan-fry it until it is very golden and crisp on the top and bottom, 2 to 3 minutes per side. Transfer to a paper towel to drain.

3 . Turn the heat to medium-low. Add the onion to the remaining oil and cook, stirring occasionally, until the onion has softened, 5 to 6 minutes. Season with a pinch of salt. Add the garlic, ginger, turmeric, coriander, cumin, and pepper flakes and cook for another minute or so.

4 . Chop the preserved lemon so finely that it is almost a paste and add it to the pan. Pour in the coconut milk and stir to combine. Season with salt and bring this to a simmer. Simmer this broth until the coconut milk has reduced by nearly half, 8 to 10 minutes.

5 . Return the tempeh to the pan and give everything a mix to get it all creamy and coated. Taste and season with salt and black pepper, as needed.

6 . In a small bowl, toss the herbs with the preserved lemon brine to make a quick herb salad. You'll have extra curry sauce around the tempeh, so I like to spread a layer on top of the flatbread, making a tempeh pizza of sorts. Top with the lemony, herby salad and eat with a fork and knife.

TOFU CUTLETS & A BRIGHT SUMMERY SALAD

Serves 3

There is no greater joy than a cutlet. Not only is the name adorable (cutlet is one letter away from cute-let), they are a crispy, light, blank canvas of fried. Pull out this bread crumb–coated tofu recipe and use it with whatever you want. It goes marvelously under the Tamari Heirloom Tomatoes (page 121) or the Spring Peas & Edamame with Greeny Tahini (page 125). No matter what salad you're making, assemble it while the cute-let drains after frying. In the summer, I make this peach and tomato salad, whose juices drip down into the tofu's crispy breading; which might be my second-greatest joy (but who's really counting?).

1 (16-ounce) block extra-firm tofu

2 or 3 very small heirloom tomatoes, various colors, plus more as needed

1 small peach

1 teaspoon Aleppo pepper flakes

1 garlic clove, grated

1 tablespoon honey

1 tablespoon apple cider vinegar or fresh lemon juice

1 cup torn tender fresh herbs, such as basil, mint, parsley

Diamond Crystal kosher salt

Extra-virgin olive oil

1 cup panko bread crumbs

⅓ cup whole-wheat flour

½ cup milk or plant-based milk

3 tablespoons soy sauce

3 tablespoons rice vinegar

Neutral oil, such as avocado, for frying

1. Slice the tofu horizontally into three large rectangular pieces, each a little less than 1 inch thick. Press the tofu (see page 207).

2. Meanwhile, cut the tomatoes into large pieces and slice the peach. In a large bowl, whisk together the Aleppo pepper, garlic, honey, and vinegar to form a dressing at the bottom of the bowl. Add the tomatoes, peach, and herbs and toss. Season with a pinch of salt, then drizzle in 1 tablespoon olive oil. Add this bowl to the fridge, while you prepare the tofu.

3. To fry the tofu, set up a dredging station with four bowls: Place the panko in one shallow dish and mix in ¼ teaspoon salt. Place the flour in a second shallow dish. Pour the milk into a wide bowl. In the fourth bowl, whisk together the soy sauce and rice vinegar.

4. Take the pressed tofu and quickly dip each side in the soy sauce–vinegar mixture. Immediately transfer each piece to the flour and dip to coat each side. Transfer each piece to the milk and then to the panko. Flip to coat each cutlet fully in the bread crumbs.

5. Set a large high-sided sauté pan over medium heat and heat the avocado oil to 350°F on a thermometer. Add the first cutlet and fry until nicely golden on both sides, 3 to 4 minutes per side. Transfer to a paper towel to drain. Repeat with the remaining cutlets.

6. To serve, take the salad out of the fridge. It will have gathered more juices in the bottom of the bowl during the time it sat, so give everything a big mix to combine again. Pile the salad generously on top of the tofu, adding more herbs as you prefer. Drizzle with any remaining juice left in the salad bowl and serve.

BLACK GARLIC SEA BASS WITH PICKLE-Y GINGER SLAW

Serves 4

Black garlic is garlic that is aged to the point where the cloves are, well, black. This aging occurs in a dark, moist environment for a matter of weeks—or in your Instant Pot at home. I don't recommend this, unless you love a solid three weeks of garlic scent in your living room . . . for ambiance. Black garlic cloves are soft enough to mash, and its sharpness mellows to a smoky, almost sweet flavor that glosses over the top of a crispy-skinned bass in a punchy, savory glaze. I suggest hunting down the whole-clove form of black garlic from a specialty grocer or food supply store, because the dried spice versions don't have the same sticky, smoky je ne sais quoi.

5 tablespoons rice vinegar

1 teaspoon granulated sugar

Diamond Crystal kosher salt

1 bird's eye chili, thinly sliced

¼ cup fresh cilantro leaves, finely chopped

2 tablespoons thinly sliced fresh ginger

3 or 4 small radishes, any type or color, thinly sliced

2 tablespoons mirin

1 tablespoon plus 1 teaspoon red miso paste

4 black garlic cloves

1 tablespoon dark brown sugar

4 skin-on black sea bass fillets (4 to 6 ounces each)

1 tablespoon grapeseed oil

1 tablespoon salted butter

Steamed rice, for serving

1 . In a small bowl, whisk together 3 tablespoons of the vinegar, the granulated sugar, 1 teaspoon salt, the chili, and cilantro. Add the ginger and radishes and toss to create a pickle-y slaw. Cover and let this sit in the fridge, while you prepare the fish.

2 . In a medium bowl, use a mini spatula to mix together the remaining 2 tablespoons vinegar, the mirin, miso, black garlic, and the brown sugar. Use the spatula to mash the garlic cloves with the mixture until smooth.

3 . Pat the fish dry and season with salt on both sides.

4 . Set a large skillet over medium-high heat and wait until you can add a few drops of water and they form balls that bounce around the pan; this will make it so your pan is nearly nonstick. Turn the heat to medium and let it cool for a few minutes, then add the oil and butter and swirl to combine. Gently place the fish skin-side down in the pan and cook, undisturbed, until the skin is very brown and the flesh is almost fully opaque, 6 to 8 minutes. Flip and cook for another minute to cook through, then remove the fish from the pan.

5 . Turn the heat to medium-low, discard any crispy bits, and add the black garlic sauce. Cook, stirring constantly, until the mixture is reduced to a thick glaze—where you can run a spatula through the center of the pan and see the bottom for a few seconds. Using a brush or a spoon, generously coat each fillet with a portion of the glaze.

6 . Give the pickle-y salad a few tosses to get all the juices together and serve alongside the bass and steamed white rice.

BOYFRIEND SALMON

Serves 4

There's Ina Garten's famous Engagement Roast Chicken recipe—and then there's this less-intense, equally useful boyfriend salmon. Think: St. Louis–style barbecue sauce (my hometown, thank you) meets crispy-skin salmon and a cooking technique that looks impressive but is nearly impossible to mess up. It's the salmon to get your boyfriend down with salmon. It will at least lock him in for four more dates because he'll think you're a fish genius. (But also, gender is a construct, and cooking for a man is antiquated, so if you're in the mood to fight the patriarchy, just make this salmon for yourself.)

1 tablespoon grapeseed oil

4 skin-on salmon fillets
(about 1 pound)

Diamond Crystal kosher salt

Freshly ground black pepper

1 tablespoon fish sauce

1 tablespoon tomato paste

1 tablespoon apple cider
vinegar

1 tablespoon dark brown sugar

½ teaspoon black mustard
seeds

⅛ teaspoon cayenne pepper

2 tablespoons unsalted butter

½ small red onion, thinly sliced

1 . Preheat the oven to 450°F.

2 . Set a large ovenproof pan over medium heat and add the grapeseed oil. Season the salmon with salt and black pepper on both sides and place skin-side down in the pan. Cook until the skin gets golden around the edges, 3 to 4 minutes. Transfer the pan to the oven and bake for 7 to 9 minutes, or until it reaches an internal temperature of 135°F.

3 . Meanwhile, in a small bowl, whisk together the fish sauce, tomato paste, vinegar, brown sugar, mustard seeds, cayenne, and ¼ cup water.

4 . Set a medium pan over medium heat and add the butter. Let it melt and begin to brown slightly, 2 to 3 minutes. Add the onion and cook until softened, 3 to 4 minutes. Pour in the fish sauce mixture. Turn off the heat and stir to combine, seasoning with a generous pinch of salt.

5 . When the salmon is out of the oven, gently flip it into the pan with the sauce, exposing the crispy skin side. Transfer to a plate, taking a scoop of sauce for each fillet, and pooling any additional sauce around and on top of the salmon.

WHITEFISH PEPERONATA

Serves 2

Peperonata is an Italian bell pepper side dish, traditionally fish-less, but wow, is it so good when it's fish-filled. Stewed sweet peppers cook down in olive oil, with a touch of capers and vinegar to make it bright and briny. The fish finishes on top, making dinner happen in one pan in a matter of minutes. Whitefish, although sometimes passed over for being boring, is very easy to get where I live, especially varieties like flounder, cod, and skate, all of which work well with this recipe. It's a 30-minute, vegetable-packed dinner, and the leftovers make fantastic toast the next day.

Extra-virgin olive oil

2 large bell peppers, assorted colors, cored, seeded, and sliced

1 small red onion, thinly sliced

Diamond Crystal kosher salt

3 garlic cloves, grated

1 tablespoon nonpareil capers in salt brine, drained and chopped

1 tablespoon red wine vinegar

¼ cup packed fresh basil leaves, torn

¼ cup packed fresh flat-leaf parsley leaves, finely chopped

12 ounces whitefish, such as flounder, cod, halibut, mahi-mahi, or another fish of choice, divided into 2 pieces

Freshly ground black pepper

Bread or steamed rice, for serving

1. Set a large pan with a tightly fitted lid over medium heat and add ¼ cup olive oil. Add the bell peppers and onion and cook, stirring occasionally, until both have softened significantly, 12 to 15 minutes. Season with salt.

2. Add the garlic, capers, vinegar, basil, and parsley and stir, cooking for another 5 minutes or until you cannot smell the sharpness of any raw garlic anymore.

3. Season each fish fillet with salt and black pepper. Nestle each fillet on top of the peppers, cover, and steam until the fish is opaque all the way through, 4 to 5 minutes (the timing will vary based on the thickness of your fish, so keep an eye on it).

4. Uncover and remove from the heat. Scoop the fish along with some peperonata onto two plates. This is wonderful served with fresh bread or fluffy rice.

SMOKY SCALLOPS OVER CRISPY QUINOA

Serves 2 to 4

The secret to good scallops is a hard, fearless sear, which I learned the hard, fearful way. I served my culinary classmates blond, possibly undercooked, scallops, but hey, no one died. (I swear I know what I'm doing now!) If you're a beginner cook, stay with me, because scallops are one of the best starter proteins. Their disk shape browns evenly and is easy to flip with tongs, and they cook so quickly—once your pan is hot enough. We'll make a lemony pan sauce in the scallop juices that creates a flavor that reminds me of summertime crab boils. And the contrast of crispy quinoa with the buttery scallops is Texture 101.

1 pound dry-packed scallops

Diamond Crystal kosher salt

Freshly ground black pepper

2 tablespoons neutral oil, such as grapeseed oil

2 garlic cloves, smashed and peeled

2 tablespoons salted butter

½ small red onion, thinly sliced

1 teaspoon smoked paprika

¼ teaspoon red pepper flakes

2 tablespoons fresh lemon juice (about ½ lemon)

1 cup tender fresh herbs, such as parsley, mint, dill, chives

1 cup Crispy Quinoa (page 43)

1. Pat the scallops dry with a paper towel and pull off any of the crescent-shaped pieces on their sides. (This is the muscle piece that can toughen as it cooks, but it's easy to remove.) Season the scallops with salt and black pepper on both sides.

2. Set a large pan over medium heat and add the neutral oil, letting it heat up to where it is a little wispy and smoky. Working in two batches, sear the scallops until dark and golden on both sides, 3 to 4 minutes per side. For each batch, add 1 of the garlic cloves and 1 tablespoon of the butter. When the butter has melted, tilt the pan and baste the scallops for 30 seconds. Transfer to a platter and repeat with the second batch.

3. Scrape away any remaining scallop bits from the pan and remove the garlic cloves but leave any excess butter and oil. Turn the heat to medium-low, add the onion, and cook until softened, 4 to 5 minutes. Season with a pinch of salt and add the paprika, pepper flakes, ¼ cup water, and 1 tablespoon of the lemon juice. Swirl to combine, then bring to a simmer. Let the sauce reduce by half. Set aside.

4. In a small bowl, tear apart the herbs and toss with the remaining 1 tablespoon lemon juice and season with salt.

5. To serve, scatter the quinoa on a serving platter, top with the scallops, spoon on the sauce, and top with the herb salad.

MY DAUGHTER'S KITCHEN

Kitchens tend to be matriarchal territory. Grandmothers have taught daughters to cook, who then have taught their daughters—and so on and so forth. But for me, it's impossible to talk about cooking without talking about my dad.

I have a series of recipes and videos called My Daughter's Kitchen, where I prepare the foods I hope to make for my future daughter and speak to how I didn't really grow up in a food family. While all this is true, there was one really great cook in my family. My father, a man of Cajun descent who was dubbed an "everything man" by his friends, because his hobbies spanned everything from fly-fishing to orchestra and the kitchen was only a fraction of the places where his loud voice and boisterous personality took over. His cooking was well-known by neighbors, coworkers, acquaintances, and even the plumber he'd once befriended in the 45 minutes he'd been in our house. He'd cook for big, lively dinner parties before I was old enough to see over the table, and it smelled *amazing*.

He was the one who served me and my siblings bacon-wrapped water chestnuts; he was the one who let us watch as he cooked a roux until it was black; yet he was gone before he could teach us any of it. Maybe our loss of being a food family was also tied to our loss of him. Maybe we mourned in a different way.

And maybe, in talking about my daughter's kitchen, I was really talking about his daughter's kitchen. My kitchen. A place we built together.

I remember when he bought me my first swordfish steak, unwrapping the paper and saying I would like it because I loved flank steak. Apparently, they were similar. And as always, he was right. He seared it in a cast-iron skillet and let it rest so that it sliced like butter. Now I can't think of cooking swordfish any other way.

I say I don't come from a food family, but that's not entirely true. He was our food family, and he's why I'm so invested in building my own. And while it probably doesn't hold a candle to his swordfish, I hope he would have liked my recipe (page 225). It *did* come from his daughter's kitchen, after all.

SWORDFISH WITH BLISTERED CORN & PEACH SALSA

Serves 4

Swordfish is my steak—the filet mignon of fish. It's no secret that's how a lot of people see it, too, since it looks like a thick slab of meat (and can char like one, too). But what's nice about swordfish is you don't need to mess with it too much to make it great—a few minutes in a cast-iron skillet is all it asks for. I know there's a bit of hesitation around swordfish for its higher levels of mercury, so like filet mignon, I don't recommend eating swordfish every night. It's a special occasion fish, meant for a special occasion blistered corn salsa to go with it.

¼ cup pumpkin seeds

Extra-virgin olive oil

2 cups fresh corn kernels (about 2 large ears)

1 medium peach, diced

Diamond Crystal kosher salt

½ small red onion, diced

1 serrano pepper, seeded and thinly sliced

⅓ cup fresh mint leaves, chiffonade cut (see page 30)

⅓ cup fresh cilantro leaves, finely chopped

3 tablespoons fresh lime juice (about 2 limes)

Freshly ground black pepper

4 swordfish fillets (about 1 pound)

2 tablespoons avocado oil, for frying

1. Set a large cast-iron skillet over medium heat and add the pumpkin seeds. Toast, stirring occasionally, until golden and fragrant, 7 to 8 minutes. Remove them from the pan, coarsely chop, and add them to a medium bowl.

2. Keep the skillet over medium heat, add a drizzle of olive oil to coat the bottom, and add the corn and peaches. Let both cook, undisturbed, until blackened spots start to appear, about 4 minutes. Give the pan a few stirs with a spatula and cook, undisturbed, for another 4 minutes. Transfer the corn and peaches to the bowl with the pumpkin seeds and season with a pinch of salt. Wipe out the pan.

3. To the bowl with the corn and peaches, add the onion, serrano pepper, mint, cilantro, lime juice, and 1 tablespoon olive oil. Season with salt and a few cracks of black pepper and toss to create the salsa.

4. Pat the swordfish fillets dry with a paper towel and season with salt and black pepper. Place the cast-iron skillet back over medium heat and add the avocado oil. Give the oil a few minutes to heat up, then add the swordfish and cook until the internal temperature is at least 135°F, 3 to 4 minutes on each side. Set the swordfish aside and let it rest for 5 minutes.

5. To serve, top each fillet with a healthy helping of corn salsa. If you have any salsa left over, break out the chips.

LITTLENECK CLAMS WITH PRESERVED LEMON BUTTER

Serves 4

Clams, like scallops, are an unexpectedly great entry-level protein. The most intimidating part is making sure they're fully scrubbed clean, which is a task I do in my salad spinner, because it's multifunctional. I cover the clams with cold water, give a few scrubs with a brush, drain, and repeat. After a good clean and a good steam, clams release their briny juices right into the spicy, beany broth we have waiting for them. I serve this with grilled sourdough to soak up the broth, of which there should be none left by the time you're done with it.

½ preserved lemon, homemade (see page 39) or store-bought, finely chopped

2 scallions, thinly sliced, white and green parts kept separate

2 tablespoons salted butter, at room temperature

Extra-virgin olive oil

4 large slices sourdough bread, each at least 1 inch thick

1 (15-ounce) can white beans, drained and rinsed

1 serrano pepper, thinly sliced

2 garlic cloves, sliced

½ cup vegetable broth

1 tablespoon fresh lemon juice (about ½ lemon)

2 dozen littleneck clams, rinsed and scrubbed

Diamond Crystal kosher salt

Freshly ground black pepper

1. In a small bowl, mix together the preserved lemon, 1 tablespoon of the green parts of the scallions, and the butter and set aside.

2. Set a deep sauté pan with a fitted lid over medium heat and add 2 tablespoons olive oil. Grill all the bread until golden on both sides, about 2 minutes per side. Transfer to a plate.

3. Add another 2 tablespoons olive oil and the beans to the pan and cook undisturbed, letting the oil sizzle around the beans, for 1 minute. Push the beans to one side of the pan and add the white parts of the scallions, the serrano pepper, and garlic to the other side. Cook, stirring occasionally, until the garlic is lightly browned, 2 to 3 minutes. Stir everything together to combine.

4. Add the broth, lemon juice, and clams. Cover and let the clams steam until they open, 5 to 8 minutes. If any clams remain unopened, discard them; they aren't suitable for eating.

5. Uncover and taste the broth. Season with salt and black pepper to taste, although it shouldn't need much. Spoon in dots of the preserved lemon butter (ideally, right into the clam shells) and cover for another 30 seconds to 1 minute to let it melt into the clam broth.

6. Scoop onto the toasts and garnish with the remaining scallion greens.

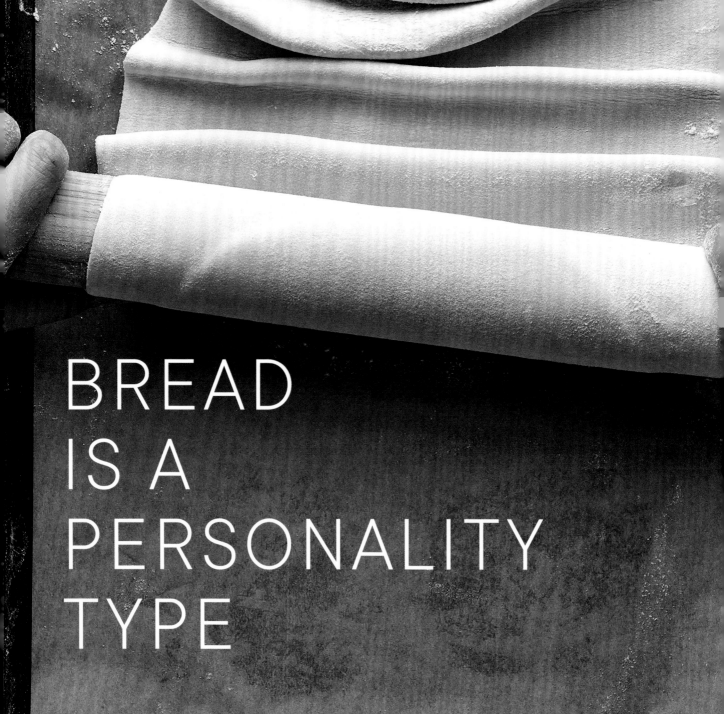

BREAD
IS A
PERSONALITY
TYPE

I OFTEN JOKE THAT ONE DAY I'LL RETIRE TO LIVE A LIFE OF BREAD, but the more I joke about it, the more I really do dream about it. A tiny cozy house, a wall of sourdoughs for sale, me in a cute little apron? It calls to me. Bread is my personality type.

People say there are cooks and there are bakers—two different breeds—which is an idea I don't subscribe to, but there is admittedly a certain fixation that comes with making bread. You have to be slightly in the trenches to be a baker, where patience, care, and attention go a long way. Certain breads are learned over time and tests, like the sourdough on page 235, which will give you all the instructions to tackle (and master) your first rounds. Other breads are less intensive but still offer the satisfaction of kneading and working with dough, like the More Butter Than Rolls (page 238), where you hand-shape each individual pocket and are rewarded later with pillowy, butter-dripping goodness (and a kitchen that smells *amazing*).

And then there are fast and sustaining breads, like the Broiled Yogurt Flatbreads (page 245) or the fun and layered Ripple Bread (page 241), both meant for rolling out, quickly baking, and dipping through everything delicious. You can also do this with the Sweet Potato Focaccia (page 246), because I'll never regulate which breads you can and cannot dip.

Remember that bread *wants* to be worked with. It wants to be handled, shaped, pressed, poked, and stretched just enough. It takes feeling, intuition, and attention to detail. In that way, it's like cooking, where the more you repeat a recipe, the more it gives back to you. So, when people look at me and say, "Oh, I'm not a baker; I'm more of a cook," I like to reply that there's more in common than you might think.

LOW-DISCARD SOURDOUGH STARTER

Makes 1 very powerful starter

In order to make sourdough bread, you need a sourdough starter: a small batch of flour and water that has fermented to the point that it can leaven bread all on its own. But in order to create a ripe, ready-for-baking starter, you need to "feed" it fresh flour and then discard up to half of it the next day. The idea here is that you're creating a lively, good bacteria–filled environment, where yeast feeds on flour, helped out by water, that'll ultimately help your loaf of sourdough rise and have great flavor.

It always bothers me how much flour is wasted when I feed—and discard—my starter. Depending on the size of your starter, it can be around 1 cup of flour each time. A professional baker's big worry is that a small amount of flour doesn't have enough sugar for the starter's yeast to feed on, but I've never had that issue with this recipe. I start with the smallest amount of flour possible and only begin discarding on the fourth day. Sourdough starters are all about visual cues (it's "ripe" when it's nearly doubled in size and very bubbly), so I included some photos (see page 233), which I hope help along your first sourdough starter journey.

Whole-wheat flour, various amounts

Unbleached all-purpose flour, various amounts

Day 1 On the first day, mix 15 grams whole-wheat flour with 15 grams cool water in a 16-ounce clear glass jar. Ensure that the flour is fully saturated; it should be the consistency of a paste. Cover it loosely with a cloth or lid (leave it cracked so the starter can breathe) and set it on your counter for 24 hours.

Day 2 Uncover the lid on day two and add 30 grams all-purpose flour and 30 grams cool water. The swap of flours is to prevent any overgrowth of bacteria. The whole wheat kickstarts fermentation, but switching to all-purpose helps control it. Mix again, cover, and store in the same place for another 24 hours.

Day 3 On the third day when you tip the jar to the side, you should see some bubbles clinging to the edges. The smell will be sour, slightly yeasty. Add 90 grams all-purpose flour and 90 grams cool water to the jar. Mix to combine. Cover and let rest for another 24 hours.

Recipe continues

Day 4   Day four is where you'll see a lot of bubbles; it will look fizzy, it will smell yeasty, but it's a long way off from being ready. Now we start to discard to prevent overgrowth. Pour out 90 grams of the starter into a fresh jar, discarding the rest. Add 90 grams of all-purpose flour and 90 grams cool water, mix, and cover.

Days 5 to 7   Days five through seven are where a bit of patience comes in, because this starter needs a bit of space to grow and breathe. Don't feed it until it starts to look bubbly, almost fizzy, slightly foamy, and very liquidy. If it's the summer and the starter sits in a warm room, this might happen by day six, but if it's winter or in a colder space, it might take up to day seven or eight.

Day 6, 7, or 8   When it is time to feed again, pour 70 grams of starter into a fresh jar, discarding the rest. Then add 70 grams of all-purpose flour and 70 grams water. Mix and let sit overnight.

At this point, the starter should begin to grow and fall, meaning you'll see it bubble to nearly twice its size, then collapse back to its original level, usually within 12 hours. If you see line marks on the side of the starter jar, you'll know your starter has been rising. If you need extra assurance, put a rubber band around the jar to mark when the starter has just been fed. If it rises at least 50 percent above that line, it means it is ready for use. Use your starter when it is at peak ripeness, meaning the bubbles have grown all the way to their highest point, which can sometimes be up to double in size (see photo). I refer to this as activated starter.

Maintenance   To maintain your starter, discard all but 70 grams of starter daily. Refeed with 70 grams all-purpose flour and 70 grams cool water. Mix and cover loosely and let it rest for 24 hours. Repeat to replenish it as needed.

NOTE: You can also "hibernate" your starter by keeping it in the fridge. First, feed your starter, then transfer it to the fridge. It can stay there for 1 to 2 weeks before it needs to be refed. If you're in the mood to bake, feed your hibernated starter right out of the fridge. If it's rising, you can bake that day, but some starters might need a few feedings after hibernation to get them to full strength.

A NOTE ON GRAMS

On my website I had to start adding a caveat paragraph to my baking recipes about why I prefer to write them in grams. The simplest reason is that it's way more accurate, not to mention more universally available. (For any international friends reading this, hi! And thank you for agreeing with me.) A measuring cup is a great tool, but while you might pack your flour the same way every time, there's still a high chance that the amount of flour varies in weight by at least 20 to 35 grams, and that's a big difference!

I recommend getting a small digital scale, which costs $15 to $20, but the price is worth the headache of cleaning sourdough starter out of a measuring cup every day, trust me.

MY SIMPLEST SOURDOUGH

Makes 1 small loaf

This recipe will work with any powerful starter, but you can also start one from scratch with my method on page 231.

There are many ways to make sourdough bread, but my simplest method is also the one that's designed to get you as close to bakery results at home. The key to the gluten development process is time and super-gentle handling. Nothing too fancy here. Just a few folds and a lot of waiting time. But the patience gets you a dark bake with a thick and crispy crust, big round bubbles, and a tangy, chewy texture that I can't get enough of. I'll always say once you go sourdough, you won't go back.

1 cup / 234g water, between 90° and 95°F

½ cup / 60g activated starter (see page 231)

1½ cups / 210g bread flour

¾ cup / 90g whole-wheat flour

2 teaspoons / 6g Diamond Crystal kosher salt

Rice flour, for dusting

1 . In a large bowl, mix together the water and starter. Use your hand to ensure the starter is fully dissolved and the water appears foamy.

2 . Add both flours and use your hands to mix into a shaggy dough. Cover with a damp cloth and let sit for 20 minutes.

3 . Prepare a small water bowl to the side. Sprinkle the salt over the top of the dough, then dip your working hand into the small water bowl to dampen it and prevent it from sticking to the dough. Pull one edge of the dough up until it feels taut, then fold it over the top of the dough, encasing the salt. Rotate the bowl 90 degrees and repeat with another edge. Repeat this process four or five times, until the dough completely encapsulates the salt. Dampen your hand again and pinch across the dough, pressing the salt in to combine. Rotate the bowl 180 degrees and pinch again. It's repetitive, yes, but enjoy the process. Dampen your hand and repeat the folding and pinching process, until you feel as if the salt is well incorporated (see photos on page 233).

4 . Using your hand in a scoop shape, scoop underneath the dough and lift it out of the bowl, then gently place it back in the bowl, letting the edges fold under each other, rotating the bowl 180 degrees each time. Do this a few times, until the dough looks like a smooth mound. Cover the bowl with a damp cloth and let sit for 30 minutes.

Recipe continues

5 . Lightly dampen a work surface and transfer the dough onto it. Using both hands, lift the dough off the work surface, then gently slap and fold it onto itself. Rotate your hands 90 degrees, then lift and repeat again. Do this a few times, until the dough is in a very tight mound. Cover with a damp towel and let sit for 30 minutes.

6 . Repeat this same step 30 minutes later. Then cover and repeat again after another 30 minutes. Transfer the dough to a clear bowl, where you can watch it rise.

7 . Cover and let the dough rise (or as the professionals say, bulk ferment) until just under double in size, with a slightly domed top and some bubbles on the sides of the bowl and just a few on the surface, 4 to 5 hours.

8 . Transfer the dough to a lightly floured work surface. Pull one edge of the dough up until it feels taut, then fold it over the top of the dough, shaping the dough into an upside-down ball. Rotate the dough 90 degrees and repeat with another edge. When you have all the edges pinched in, use a bench scraper to flip the dough over so it looks like a tight ball. Cup your hands around the edges and gently pull the dough toward you, letting the seam of the dough grip against the work surface and tighten up. Rotate and repeat a few times. Let it sit for 20 to 30 minutes.

9 . Prepare a proofing basket with a liberal dusting of rice flour. Flip the dough back over to reveal the seam. Gently tug at the edges to form a big rectangle. Fold one-third of the dough over itself, then the opposite third, pinch the edges down the center, then roll the dough from the top to the bottom, making a tight oblong loaf.

10 . Scoop up the loaf with your bench scraper, giving the seam one last seal, and flip, seam-side up, into the proofing basket. Cover with a loose plastic bag, punch a few air holes in it, and set this to proof in the fridge for 24 to 48 hours.

11 . When it's time to bake, set a Dutch oven on the center rack of the oven and preheat the oven to 500°F.

12 . When the Dutch oven has been preheated for about 45 minutes, flip the loaf seam-side down onto a piece of parchment paper. Use a razor or sharp knife to score the top in one long cut down the center. I score about ⅓ inch (1 cm) deep. Immediately transfer to the Dutch oven and cover.

13 . Bake, covered, for 20 minutes.

14 . Uncover and bake until it's deeply burnished, 5 to 7 minutes.

15 . Let it cool for 2 hours before cutting—it may feel impossible, but I believe in you.

BAKER'S PERCENTAGE

This recipe is for one loaf, but it follows the rule of baker's percentage. Baker's percentage for a bread recipe considers the total weight of the flour to be 100%, and all the other ingredients are then expressed as a percentage compared to that total. So if you are making a bread loaf that uses 100 grams of flour and 80 grams of water, that means the recipe uses an 80% water amount in the dough.

My preferred sourdough baker's percentage is:

100% flour / 78% water / 20% starter / 2% salt

Meaning if I wanted to make a loaf that uses only 100 grams of flour, my recipe would look like:

100 grams flour / 78 grams water / 20 grams starter / 2 grams salt

It's a bit of a math equation to master, but baker's percentage is a golden rule of sourdough. Once you understand it, you can scale a recipe up or down as you prefer.

MORE BUTTER THAN ROLLS

Makes 21 rolls

If you like little rounds of pillowy dough snuggled up against one another so that butter pools in the crevices, you've found the right page. This is my version of Parker House rolls that takes some liberties with a mix of all-purpose flour and whole-wheat flour. The term "more butter than roll" might not be completely accurate, but after brushing butter on top, it sure does feel that way.

8 tablespoons / 113g salted butter

1½ cups / 360g whole milk

¼ cup / 55g sugar

1 tablespoon plus 2½ teaspoons / 12g active dry yeast

3 cups / 420g all-purpose flour

1½ cups /210g whole-wheat flour

1 tablespoon / 11g Diamond Crystal kosher salt

1 teaspoon flaky salt

1 . In a small measuring cup, melt 6 tablespoons / 90g of the butter. Add the milk, 6 tablespoons / 90g warm water, and the sugar. Either by microwaving in 30-second increments or by cooking over low heat on the stove, bring this mixture to between 100° and 115°F.

2 . Sprinkle the yeast over the milk mixture and gently stir it in. Let it sit until it's foamy on top, about 5 minutes.

3 . In a stand mixer fitted with the dough hook, combine both flours and the kosher salt. Pour in the yeasty milk and mix on medium speed, until the dough pulls from the sides of the bowl, 7 to 8 minutes.

4 . Use a damp hand to pull the dough away from the hook. Transfer to an oiled bowl and cover to proof until doubled in size, about 1 hour.

5 . When the dough has doubled, gently punch out any excess air. On a lightly floured countertop, portion the dough into twenty-one equal pieces (56g each). Stretch these into strips about 4 inches long, then swoop them into a loop around your knuckles, forming them into 2-inch-long oblong pieces. Nestle them 1 inch apart in a 9 by 13-inch baking dish in three rows of seven rolls in each.

6 . Cover the baking dish and let the rolls proof, until they have poofed up to the point where all their edges are touching, 1 to 1½ hours.

7 . Preheat the oven to 375°F. Bake until the rolls are golden brown, 20 to 25 minutes.

8 . Set a small pan over medium heat and brown the remaining butter, letting it melt and foam until there are deep golden-brown flecks at the bottom of the pan, 4 to 5 minutes.

9 . Remove from the oven, brush them with the brown butter and sprinkle with flaky salt. Let cool for 5 to 10 minutes before eating.

RIPPLE BREAD

Serves 4 to 6

Meet Ripple Bread, which is exactly what it sounds like. A bread I invited to layer over itself into stackable, tearable ripples. The best part of this bread is the shape. When you cut it like a pie, everyone gets a crisp, crackerlike edge and a bunch of piled-over folds in the middle. The perk of the ripples is they are primed for sauce catching and flavor holding; the other perk is that it comes out looking like an unmade bed. And I love anything that is both bed plus bread related.

1½ cups / 210g all-purpose flour, plus more for kneading

½ teaspoon Diamond Crystal kosher salt

1 teaspoon baking powder

½ cup / 100g sour cream or Greek yogurt

3 tablespoons / 45g Your Perfect Herb Oil (page 34), or any good olive oil

¼ teaspoon flaky salt

1. In a large bowl, whisk together the flour, salt, and baking powder. Add the sour cream with ¼ cup / 60g water and mix into a shaggy dough. Transfer this dough to a lightly floured surface and knead for 3 to 5 minutes to shape it into a smooth ball. Cover loosely with plastic wrap and let rest for 10 minutes.

2. Position a rack in the top of the oven and preheat it to 400°F. Line a sheet pan with parchment paper.

3. When the dough has rested, lightly dust it with flour again and use a rolling pin to roll it out into a long oval, 24 to 28 inches long and 8 to 9 inches wide. Roll this piece of dough onto your rolling pin and then transfer it to the lined sheet pan. When rolling it onto the sheet pan, let the bread drape every 2 inches in overlapping "ripples," creating a circle shape with many wrinkles.

4. Brush the top of the bread with 2 tablespoons of the herb oil, making sure to get it in all the crevices and nooks.

5. Bake until the edges of the bread are golden and crisp, 15 to 18 minutes. When it's out of the oven, brush it with the remaining 1 tablespoon oil and sprinkle on the flaky salt. Cut into triangular slices, like a pizza, and share.

BEET-PINK BRIOCHE

Makes one 9-inch loaf

I had a weekend where I was making beet-pickled deviled eggs, and the fridge was full of beets, looking lost in there. What started as a quick swap in a potato bread recipe was then tweaked and shifted into this super-soft, subtly sweet, bright-pink brioche. Think of it as a cousin to potato bread, perfect for toast and jam, or plating up as avocado toast (with beet-pickled eggs on top? It's a possibility.) The color is the draw, but the taste will win you over, since this pillowy bread needs only a slathering of butter and salt to accomplish what it set out to do: make you happy.

1 medium / 5½ ounce / 160g red beet

4 tablespoons / 57g salted butter, melted

¾ cup / 180g warm water, between 100° and 110°F

2 tablespoons / 30g sugar

2¼ teaspoons / 7g active dry yeast

3 cups / 420g all-purpose flour, plus more for shaping

2 teaspoons / 6g Diamond Crystal kosher salt

Extra-virgin olive oil, for oiling the bowl

1 large egg, for egg wash

1. Position a rack in the center of the oven and preheat it to 425°F.

2. Peel and wrap the beet in aluminum foil. Roast until soft, 35 to 45 minutes.

3. Slice the beet and add it to a blender with ⅓ cup / 80g cool water. Blend until smooth. This should yield ¾ cup / 140g beet puree; discard any extra.

4. In a small measuring cup, combine the melted butter and warm water. Whisk in the sugar and let it dissolve. Ensure the entire mixture is between 100° and 115°F before sprinkling in the yeast. Stir to combine and let sit until the yeast is foamy, about 5 minutes.

5. In a stand mixer fitted with the dough hook, combine the flour, salt, and beet puree. Pour in the yeast mixture and mix on medium-low speed until everything is just combined. Increase the speed to medium and mix until the dough starts to pull away from the sides of the bowl, 7 to 8 minutes. Use a damp hand to pull the dough from the hook and transfer it to an oiled bowl. Cover and let this proof until at least doubled in size, about 1½ hours.

6. Line the bottom and sides of a 9 by 5-inch loaf pan with parchment paper.

7. When the dough has doubled in size, punch it down and transfer it to a lightly floured surface. Gently pull the dough out into a rectangle and fold one side two-thirds of the way over, fold the other side over the top of that side, then roll the dough into a log, starting from the top narrow edge and rolling down. Transfer this, seam-side down, to the lined loaf pan. Cover it loosely with plastic wrap and let rise until at least increased in size by 50 percent, 30 minutes to 1 hour.

8 . While the bread is proofing, preheat the oven to 375°F.

9 . Whisk together the egg and brush it all over the top of the dough. Bake the brioche until it's deeply golden and domed on top, 25 to 30 minutes.

10 . Remove the pan from the oven, slide the brioche out of the pan, and let it cool completely before slicing.

BROILED YOGURT FLATBREADS

Makes 8 flatbreads

The best flatbread I've ever had has come out of an 800°F wood-fired oven, and the closest thing to replicating that at home has become my broiler. Where similar flatbread recipes are usually done on the stove, here you can do them four at a time on a large sheet pan, and they're ready in minutes. Yogurt makes these flatbreads stretchy, tender, and tangy, and while they mirror many breads from different cultures (paratha, pita, bazlama, to name a few), I chose the term flatbread so as not to minimize the details and tradition that goes into each and every type of bread those countries produce. I broil these all-purpose flatbreads anytime I know I'm going to need a sidekick for something saucy (Hottie Tomato Beans & Cashew Cream, page 39; Cinnamon-Romesco Chickpeas & Charred Greens, page 167; or Charred-Tomato Beans, page 176, to name a few), and occasionally, I'll make a batch to freeze and thaw throughout the week.

2¼ teaspoons / 7g active dry yeast

½ cup / 120g warm water, between 95° and 100°F

2 cups / 280g all-purpose flour, plus more for dusting

¾ cup / 180g whole-milk yogurt

1 teaspoon / 3g Diamond Crystal kosher salt

½ teaspoon sugar

Extra-virgin olive oil

1. In a large bowl, whisk together the yeast and warm water. Let this sit for 5 minutes until it begins to swell and get cloudy. Add the flour, yogurt, salt, and sugar and mix into a shaggy dough with your hands. Knead the dough in the bowl for 3 to 5 minutes, letting it smooth out into a ball. Cover and let rest for 30 minutes.

2. Transfer to a lightly floured surface, knead for another 2 minutes, and shape into a smooth, tight ball. Use a bench scraper to cut the dough into eight equal pieces. Loosely cover with plastic wrap and let these pieces rest for another 20 to 30 minutes.

3. Position a rack in the center of the oven and set the broiler to high.

4. Dust the pieces with a bit more flour and roll them out into thin flatbreads, about ¼ inch thick. Transfer the pieces to a large sheet pan and drizzle each side with olive oil. Rub oil all over the flatbreads to ensure they are evenly coated.

5. Broil until puffed up and golden, 2 to 3 minutes. Flip the flatbreads and repeat. Broilers are finicky, so the first time you make this recipe, keep an eye on them, as the times may vary.

SWEET POTATO FOCACCIA

Makes 1 quarter-sheet pan (8 servings)

Sweet potato makes this bread doubly soft but still with that springy focaccia chew that no other bread can compare to. The salty-sweet contrast is *chef's kiss*, and why I've grown to prefer this focaccia over my more traditional versions. Think of it as the sweet potato fry to the french fry, because both belong on the menu.

1 small / 5-ounce / 140g sweet potato

1 rounded teaspoon / 3.5g active dry yeast

1½ cups / 360g lukewarm water, between 85° and 95°F

2¾ cups / 390g bread flour

1 teaspoon / 3g Diamond Crystal kosher salt

Extra-virgin olive oil for oiling the bowl and drizzling

¼ teaspoon flaky salt

1 . Either in the microwave or in the oven, cook the sweet potato until it is softened throughout. Remove the skin, mash the potato, and set aside.

2 . In the bowl of a stand mixer fitted with the whisk attachment, whisk together the yeast and ¼ cup / 60g of the lukewarm water. Let it sit for 3 to 5 minutes or until it swells up slightly. Add the flour, kosher salt, and the remaining 1¼ cups / 300g lukewarm water.

3 . Snap on the dough hook and mix the dough on low for 2 minutes. It should look very wet, almost like batter. Add ½ cup / 115g of the mashed sweet potato and mix again until the potato is fully incorporated. Cover the bowl with a towel and let it rest for 10 minutes.

4 . Mix on medium-high speed until the dough pulls away from the sides of the bowl and is elastic enough to pull up in a long stretch, 12 to 17 minutes. It will take some time, so don't worry.

5 . Place the mixed dough in an oiled bowl. Cover this and let it rise until doubled in size, about 1 hour.

6 . When the dough is ready, add 3 tablespoons olive oil to a 9½ by 13-inch quarter-sheet pan. Rub the oil all over to coat the pan. Plop the dough in the center and use oiled fingers to pull it to the edges of the pan. It will be pretty elastic and pull back but don't worry about that. Let it rest for 5 to 10 minutes to let the gluten relax, then pull the relaxed dough out to the edges. Cover with oiled plastic wrap or a loose-fitting lid and let the dough rise until it has bubbled to the top of the sheet pan, about 1 hour.

7 . Preheat the oven to 425°F.

8 . When the dough has risen, drizzle with at least 2 more tablespoons of olive oil and use your fingers to dimple the dough all over. Sprinkle with the flaky salt and bake until golden brown, 20 to 25 minutes.

9 . Slice into eight rectangles, each approximately 3¼ by 4¾ inches in size, and serve warm.

END WITH SOMETHING SWEET

DESSERTS ARE THE MOST FANTASTICAL, WHIMSICAL THINGS. When I started to cook, desserts were the easiest recipes to play with—I'd mix and build flavors just to see what would happen. Haldhi doodh cookies? Done. A rum-raisin crème brûlée? Might as well try it. It's the best place to play around, because if something goes wrong, there's always ice cream in the fridge as a reliable backup. This reckless experimenting later shifted to my savory cooking, teaching me to lean into unexpected combinations for the fun of it (see the Brown Butter Tahini on Any Noodle on page 199 for a rousing success, because that was definitely modeled after cookies). But savory aside, I always need to end the day (or meal) with something sweet.

Here, I've gathered my favorite inventions in one sugary, buttery chapter, from the Green Tea Coffee Cake (page 269) that is my excuse for cake for breakfast, to the Tamarind-Date Bars (page 257) that fulfill my need for a classy version of Fig Newtons. And while my favorite types of desserts are playful and new, some traditionalists slip in, like the Berries & Cherries under Corn Bread Cakes (page 273), and the Scooped Pear Sticky Toffee Pudding in Mugs (page 258), which proves that I'm an eighty-year-old British man stuck in a thirty-year-old woman's body.

I aim for all these desserts to be as achievable as they are fun, with simple preparations that lead to big flavor payoffs. This is a chapter for unabashed sweet tooths, but it's also a place where I hope to encourage you to play and invent your own desserts with abandon . . . with a freezer full of backup ice cream.

OBSESSIVE CHOCOLATE CHIP COOKIE BEHAVIOR

In the spring of 2023, I had the brilliant idea to break down famous chocolate chip cookie recipes into percentages. Not the baker's percentage (see page 237 for more on that) but inspired by the concept. Meaning, if the weight of the cookie dough in total is 100 percent, what share of the recipe is butter? What percentage is brown sugar? I was trying to answer the ever-elusive question: What makes the perfect chocolate chip cookie? Because for a recipe that revolves around only seven to eight ingredients, it felt too obvious not to explore.

The thesis, however, is flawed. It's impossible to find the universal "best" chocolate chip cookie because we're all going to like a different type. So instead of debating what is the best recipe, I wanted to see why each recipe does what it does.

In my research, I saw cookies that called for reverse creaming, some that needed 72 hours to chill, and others that used a food processor. But the main thing I learned while baking through countless CCCs is that while techniques can make teeny, tiny changes, the biggest impact comes from the ingredient ratios.

Here, I've created a chart, starting with the percentage ratios of the Nestlé Toll House chocolate chip recipe, followed by an average of the "best" chocolate chip cookie recipes on the internet. Next are the average percentages of all the cookies I baked that gave me a thin and crisp result (like from the famed Tate's Bake Shop), and then a column that averages the cookie recipes I baked that gave me tall, dense, and domed cookies (similar to New York's Chip City or Levain Bakery cookies). The last column is the percentage of my favorite cookie and the recipe I developed for this book, where you sub out the egg for sour cream, yielding an irresistibly soft center. You can find this recipe on page 252, but I wanted to show how my favorite ratio compared to the classics.

INGREDIENT	NESTLÉ TOLL HOUSE	THE BEST CHOCOLATE CHIP COOKIE AVERAGE	A THIN & CRISPY COOKIE	A TALL & CAKEY COOKIE	MY KIND OF CHOCOLATE CHIP COOKIE
Flour	23.13%	20.94%	20.47%	34.00%	29.44%
Salt	0.29%	0.42%	0.73%	0.52%	0.38%
Baking powder	0.00%	0.00%	0.00%	0.59%	0.76%
Baking soda	0.29%	0.42%	0.73%	0.00%	0.00%
Butter	16.59%	17.70%	20.56%	16.70%	21.46%
Brown sugar	11.75%	20.94%	20.47%	14.78%	7.60%
White sugar	12.11%	5.24%	9.10%	7.39%	20.89%
Egg	10.28%	7.33%	6.10%	9.90%	0.00%
Egg yolks	0.00%	8.38%	0.00%	0.00%	0.00%
Additional	0.00%	0.00%	0.00%	0.00%	7.98%
Vanilla	0.59%	0.84%	1.36%	0.59%	0.76%
Chocolate	24.96%	17.80%	20.47%	15.52%	10.73%

It's . . . a lot of numbers. But if you look closely, you will see that tiny changes in ingredients change a cookie's texture/composition. A high-fat/low-sugar/low-flour cookie spreads thin with a cakey chew, while a high-fat/high-sugar/low-flour cookie is what gets snap-apart crisp. Low-fat/low-sugar/high-flour cookies are the huge cakelike domes you see at certain bakeries, and eggless cookies are uniformly thin and soft with crinkly tops. (All these recipes used the same process: creamed butter and sugar, added wet and dry ingredients, then mixed, scooped, and baked.)

I've only scratched the surface of my chocolate chip cookie research (wasn't it fun?), but I've used my favorite percentages to develop four recipes that cover the cookies I crave on the regular. They're all slightly different, but I hope you'll trust their ratios are spot on.

EVERYONE LIKES A DIFFERENT CHOCOLATE CHIP COOKIE

I made these four cookie recipes in a handy chart because while they have similar ingredients and processes, they make wildly different results. There's a gooey brown butter one, a tall, thick rye cookie that's a nutty cousin to those made famous by Levain Bakery, an extra-thin and crispy number for dunking in milk, and my favorite, the tangy version made with sour cream. My favorite might be the outlier here, but when you replace an egg with the higher fat, slightly acidic sour cream, it takes a classic CCC and turns it into something that always has people asking for the secret ingredient.

And while I'm biased, I'm not going to call these four the Best Chocolate Chip Cookies, because frankly, that's up to you. But also, these have been tirelessly and painfully tested. And they are pretty damn fantastic.

	BROWNEST BUTTER, DARKEST CHOCOLATE	TALL RYE GUY	EXTRA THIN, EXTRA CRISP	MY FAVORITE SOUR CREAM COOKIES
BUTTER	Brown 8 tablespoons / 113g salted butter. Pour it into a large bowl, transfer to the fridge for 15 minutes to let it solidify.	Brown 4 tablespoons / 57g salted butter and set aside in a small bowl to cool. In a large stand mixer, beat together 4 tablespoons / 57g room-temperature salted butter . . .	Melt 8 tablespoons / 113g salted butter and whisk in . . .	Add 8 tablespoons / 113g room-temperature salted butter to a mixer.
GRANULATED SUGAR & BROWN SUGAR	When the butter has firmed to a paste, move it to a stand mixer and add heaping ½ cup / 110g granulated sugar and ⅓ cup / 70g packed dark brown sugar. Beat with the paddle attachment on medium speed until fluffy and . . .	. . . with ½ cup / 100g packed dark brown sugar, ¼ scant cup / 50g granulated sugar, and 1 teaspoon vanilla bean paste for 2 to 3 minutes or until light and fluffy. Pour in the brown butter and mix on medium-high another 2 minutes.	. . . ⅓ cup and 1 scant tablespoon / 80g packed dark brown sugar, ⅓ cup / 80g granulated sugar . . .	Add 3 tablespoons packed / 40g light brown sugar, ½ cup / 110g granulated sugar, and 2 teaspoons vanilla extract and beat for 2 minutes.

	BROWNEST BUTTER, DARKEST CHOCOLATE	TALL RYE GUY	EXTRA THIN, EXTRA CRISP	MY FAVORITE SOUR CREAM COOKIES
EGGS (IF ANY)	Add 1 large egg, ¼ teaspoon coffee grounds, and 1 teaspoon vanilla extract. Beat again for 2 to 3 minutes or until it looks whipped and 1 shade lighter in color.	Crack in 1 large egg and mix on medium high for another minute or so.	1 egg white, and 1 teaspoon vanilla extract and whisk until combined.	Add ⅓ cup / 45g sour cream and beat until light and fluffy, 3 to 4 minutes. (This is replacing the eggs.)
FLOUR	Add 1 cup plus 1 tablespoon / 150g all-purpose flour . . .	Add 1 cup / 140g all-purpose flour, ⅔ cup / 90g dark rye flour . . .	Add ¾ cup plus 1 tablespoon / 120g all-purpose flour . . .	In a bowl, whisk together 1 cup plus 2 tablespoons / 160g all-purpose flour . . .
LEAVENER	1 teaspoon / 5g baking powder, and . . .	1½ teaspoons / 7g baking powder and . . .	1 teaspoon / 5g baking powder, and . . .	1½ teaspoons baking powder (7g) and . . .
SALT	1 teaspoon / 4g kosher salt. Mix into a sticky batter with a spatula.	1 teaspoon / 4g kosher salt. Mix on low until just combined.	1 teaspoon / 4g kosher salt, and fold into a batter with a spatula.	1 teaspoon kosher salt / 4g. Add to the mixer and mix on low until just combined.
CHOCOLATE	Chop up 3 ounces / 85g extra-dark chocolate, leaving some pieces big and some tiny, then mix them into the dough.	Chop up 1.7 ounces / 50g semisweet chocolate and 1.7 ounces / 50g milk chocolate and mix them into the dough.	Chop up 3 ounces / 85g semisweet chocolate and mix them into the dough..	Chop up 2 ounces / 57g semisweet chocolate and mix them into the dough.
SHAPE	Chill the dough for 15 minutes, then portion into eleven balls (53g each) and place on a baking sheet.	Portion into six cookies (105g each) and chill for 1 to 6 hours.	Scoop the dough into twelve drop cookies (40g each) and place on a baking sheet with enough room to spread out.	Roll the dough into fifteen equal pieces (35g each) and place on a baking sheet. Slightly press down the tops to create even baking.
BAKE	Position a rack in the center of the oven and bake at 400°F until the tops are barely golden, 8 to 10 minutes. Remove from the oven and serve as warm as you'd like.	Position a rack in the center of the oven and bake at 425°F until the edges and tops are golden, 8 to 11 minutes. It's okay if the centers still feel slightly underdone. Let cool on the pan completely so cookies fully set.	Position a rack in the center of the oven and bake at 375°F until golden throughout, 11 to 13 minutes. Let cool on the pan to achieve their ultimate crisp.	Position a rack in the center of the oven and bake at 375°F until they are cracked on top but still feel slightly underdone, 9 to 11 minutes. Give the baking sheet a few taps on the counter to flatten them and let cool on the pan until they are firm enough to transfer to a cooling rack.

WHY
UNDERDONE
IS DONE

You'll see in most of my cookie recipes (with the exception of extra-thin, extra-crisp ones), I call for you to pull them out of the oven when they still look a bit underdone. This is my biggest hack for baking a cookie with the most decadent texture and ensuring it keeps that texture for days.

When you take cookies out of the oven when they still look a bit gooey in the center, say, 2 to 3 minutes earlier than you'd normally pull them out, they cool down to a cookie with a perfectly dense center and crispy edges. This is because cookies continue to cook after you pull them out from the oven due to residual heat on the pan, so if you pull cookies when they look "finished," you're automatically overbaking them, causing them to be a bit dry and cakey when they fully cool. But if you pull out your cookies early and let them cool on the pan, in 30 minutes, they'll firm up into a dreamy consistency and earn you a perfect-texture-cookie reward.

EXTRA THIN,
EXTRA CRISP

MY FAVORITE
SOUR CREAM
COOKIES

BROWNEST
BUTTER, DARKEST
CHOCOLATE

TALL RYE
GUY

TAMARIND-DATE BARS

Makes one 9-inch round (about 12 slices)

Tamarind is technically a fruit, even though it looks like a bean, and it has a tart, sour taste. You see it used more commonly in savory dishes, but I think sweet is where it really shines. Tamarind paste (the juicy pulp extracted from a tamarind pod) reminds me of thick, sticky fig jam, which you'll see when it blends with the dates to make what feels like a dressed-up version of Fig Newtons. The crisp almond butter crust holds everything together while still melting in your mouth, which I think is a nice contrast when paired with the subtly sharp (and definitely sticky) tamarind filling.

1 cup / 140g all-purpose flour

¼ cup / 45g packed dark brown sugar

Diamond Crystal kosher salt

¾ cup / 200g almond butter

3 cups / 300g Medjool dates, pitted

¼ cup plus 1 tablespoon / 35g flaxseed meal

1 tablespoon maple syrup

1 tablespoon plus 2 teaspoons tamarind paste

½ teaspoon ground cardamom

¼ teaspoon ground cloves

½ teaspoon ground cinnamon

1. Position a rack in the center of the oven and preheat it to 350°F. Line a 9-inch round springform pan with parchment paper.

2. In a food processor, combine the flour, brown sugar, ¼ teaspoon salt, and the almond butter and pulse until a crumbly dough forms. Press this into the bottom of the lined springform pan.

3. Bake for 8 to 10 minutes or until the crust has lightened by one shade in color.

4. Meanwhile, wipe out the food processor and add the dates, ¼ cup of the flaxseed meal, the maple syrup, tamarind paste, cardamom, cloves, cinnamon, and ½ teaspoon salt. Process until a thick, sticky filling forms that you can scoop like Play-Doh.

5. Press the filling on top of the crust and evenly dust with the remaining 1 tablespoon flaxseed meal. Return to the oven and bake for another 10 minutes until the date mixture is firm and no longer sticky.

6. Remove the pan from the oven and let it cool to room temperature. Otherwise, it'll be pretty tricky to slice. When the bars have cooled, release them from the pan and slice them into even pieces.

SCOOPED PEAR STICKY TOFFEE PUDDING IN MUGS

Makes 4 large mugs

From the first time I heard the words "sticky toffee pudding," I knew it was going to be one of my favorite desserts of all time. I'm just a toffee kind of girl. The use of a food processor makes this a quick batter, with the only real instructions being "throw everything in and pulse!" The toffee topping takes a bit longer, but you can work on that while the mugs are in the oven. This could be baked in a standard 8 by 8-inch baking dish (see Note), but in mugs, it's automatically cozier. Plus, when you add a scoop of vanilla ice cream on top, you get a three-layer bite of cake, toffee, and cream in every spoonful—which, conceptually, is one of this recipe's finest achievements.

1 large Bosc pear, halved, cored, and cubed

3 tablespoons / 43g salted butter, chilled

1 teaspoon baking soda

Diamond Crystal kosher salt

⅓ cup / 73g granulated sugar

⅓ cup / 70g dark brown sugar

2 large eggs

¾ cup plus 2 tablespoons / 123g all-purpose flour

1 teaspoon vanilla extract

TOFFEE TOPPING

2 tablespoons / 28g salted butter

2 tablespoons / 25g dark brown sugar

1 tablespoon / 15ml heavy cream

Diamond Crystal kosher salt

NOTE: If you are baking this in an 8 by 8-inch pan, bake for 18 to 20 minutes.

1. Position a rack so that the tops of the mugs are 5 to 6 inches below the top of the oven and preheat the oven to 350°F.

2. In a food processor, combine half the pear, the butter, baking soda, ¼ teaspoon salt, the granulated sugar, brown sugar, eggs, flour, and vanilla. Process until the batter is just combined; there will still be some flecks of pear in there, and it'll look a bit grainy.

3. Stir in the remaining cubes of pear and evenly portion the batter into four ovenproof mugs. Any size will work, but 10- to 12-ounce mugs work best. Place these on a baking sheet and bake until the batter has set, 25 to 30 minutes. The baking time will vary, based on how deep your mugs are.

4. Meanwhile, make the toffee topping: Set a small saucepan over medium heat and add the butter and brown sugar and cook down, stirring often, until the toffee is softly bubbling, 5 to 7 minutes. Drizzle in the cream and stir to combine. Turn the heat to medium-low and cook for another 3 to 4 minutes to let the toffee thicken. Turn off the heat and stir in ¼ teaspoon salt.

5. When the mugs are set, remove them from the oven and set the oven to broil on high. Spoon 1 tablespoon of toffee over each mug, then broil until the toffee is bubbling and sticky all over, 2 to 3 minutes.

6. Remove the mugs from the oven and let them cool until they are warm to the touch. Serve with the extra toffee and a few scoops of vanilla ice cream.

EATING TIP, STYLING TIP, OR JUST A GENERAL TIP

Brownies and blondies almost always look, slice, and taste better after getting a rest in the fridge, whether a few hours or overnight. I know waiting on freshly baked blondies feels impossible, but if you have the willpower, it's worth the time to see the difference. After the blondies have been allowed to fully chill, you can trim off the edges and then slice them into picture-perfect bars, just like those in the photo here.

BLACK PEPPER CHAI BLONDIES

Makes one 8-inch square pan

My fiancé once declared he was having a "Dirty Chai summer," which I couldn't argue with, since iced lattes are delicious, even if they are just glorified adult glasses of milk. His surplus of chai ingredients soon turned into my baking ingredients, which eventually became these blondies. The best part of chai is that spicy, peppery note that usually comes from green cardamom and black pepper, but I opted for black pepper and fresh ginger, which bake with more heat than cardamom. But don't worry, the sweetness is still prominent enough that you can serve this at a party and no one will be appalled that you put black pepper on top of a blondie.

6 ounces / 170g white chocolate, chopped

8 tablespoons / 113g salted butter, cubed

1 tablespoon / 9g molasses

½ cup / 100g packed dark brown sugar

1 large egg

2 large egg yolks

2 tablespoons neutral oil, such as vegetable, canola, grapeseed

1 tablespoon / 7g vanilla extract

1 tablespoon grated fresh ginger

½ teaspoon ground cardamom

½ teaspoon ground cinnamon

½ teaspoon ground cloves

Freshly ground black pepper

1 cup plus 2 tablespoons / 160g all-purpose flour

½ teaspoon baking powder

Diamond Crystal kosher salt

1. Position a rack in the center of the oven and preheat it to 350°F. Line the bottom and sides of an 8 by 8-inch pan with parchment paper.

2. In a heatproof bowl that fits over the top of a medium pot to make a double boiler, combine the chocolate, butter, and molasses. Set the pot over medium heat and fill with 3 inches of water. Bring the water to a simmer, set the bowl over the top, and stir constantly to melt everything together. When everything is melted, move the bowl to the counter and add the brown sugar and whisk vigorously. The fat of the butter will start to separate, but that's normal.

3. In a small bowl, whisk together the whole egg, egg yolks, oil, vanilla, ginger, cardamom, cinnamon, cloves, and ½ teaspoon black pepper. Pouring very slowly and stirring constantly, gradually drizzle the egg mixture into the melted ingredients. It should seize up into a glossy batter. Add the flour, baking powder, and 1 teaspoon salt and stir together with a spatula.

4. Pour the batter into the lined pan. Tap the pan to evenly spread out the batter and top with a few cracks of black pepper. Bake until a toothpick inserted into the center comes out clean, 20 to 25 minutes.

5. It will look kind of cakey right out of the oven, so let it completely cool before serving. Throw it in the fridge for an hour or so before slicing for the ultimate blondie fudginess.

LIME-TART FRUIT ON SESAME-HALVA CRUMBLE

Serves 6

I like a good balance of nutty and tart, and this untraditional crumble takes that combination and knocks it out of the park. The jammy fruit gets a generous hit of lime juice, making it more tart than your typical fruit filling but a refreshing contrast to the buttery crumble. You don't have to make your own halva for this recipe, but I have an untraditional quick-and-dirty version included in case you can't find any in your area.

SESAME-HALVA CRUMBLE

¼ cup / 55g sugar

1 cup / 140g all-purpose flour

½ teaspoon grated lime zest (about 1 lime)

Diamond Crystal kosher salt

¼ cup / 45g tahini

4 tablespoons / 57g salted butter, chilled

2 tablespoons white sesame seeds

½ cup / 113g Quick & Dirty Halva (recipe follows)

LIME-TART FRUIT

4 cups (1½ pounds) fruit, such as cherries (pitted), berries, peaches, plums, or an assortment

¼ cup / 60ml fresh lime juice (2 to 3 juicy limes)

3 tablespoons / 45g sugar

Diamond Crystal kosher salt

10 fresh mint leaves

2 cups labneh, Greek yogurt, or whipped cream, for serving

1. Make the crumble: Position a rack in the center of the oven and preheat it to 350°F. Line a sheet pan with parchment paper.

2. In a food processor, combine the sugar, flour, lime zest, ¼ teaspoon salt, tahini, and butter and process until crumbly. Add the sesame seeds and halva and pulse a few more times, until everything is barely combined. Sprinkle the crumble onto the lined sheet pan.

3. Bake until golden, 20 to 25 minutes.

4. Prepare the lime-tart fruit: If using cherries or berries, halve them; if using peaches or plums, cut them into thin slices.

5. Set a pan over medium heat and add the fruit, lime juice, sugar, and ¼ teaspoon salt. Cook the fruit down, stirring every now and then as the sugars reduce, until you can swipe a spatula along the bottom of the pan and the fruit juices linger before falling back together, 7 to 10 minutes. The fruit should taste tart, bright, and slightly jammy. Toss in the mint and give one more mix.

6. To serve, scoop the labneh onto each plate, spoon the fruit on top, and sprinkle with the halva crumble. Drizzle any leftover fruit juices on top.

QUICK & DIRTY HALVA

Makes 1 cup

½ cup / 90g tahini

Diamond Crystal kosher salt

½ cup / 100g sugar

1. In a heatproof medium bowl, stir together the tahini and a pinch of salt and set aside.

2. Set a small saucepan over medium heat, and combine the sugar and 2 tablespoons water, stirring down any crystallization that may occur, until it is bubbling and between 235° and 245°F. As soon as it reaches that temperature, slowly pour the sugar into the tahini, stirring constantly, watching the sugar immediately harden and create a shattery texture.

3. Either chill this in the bowl you mixed it in or pour it into a rectangular silicone mold (silicone ice cube trays also work here). Chill in the fridge for at least 3 hours to set (which, yes, I know . . . but this is as quick as we can go!).

APPLE RYE GALETTE WITH VINEGAR CARAMEL

Makes 1 rye galette (8 servings)

If the words "vinegar" and "caramel" placed too close together turn you off, I am going to very quickly try to turn you back *on* by saying this is an *apple cider* vinegar caramel, and caramel is, obviously, a good friend to apples. The vinegar makes a caramel that's subtly fruity and just acidic enough to counteract any cloying sweetness that can happen when it's paired with something equally sugary (ahem, fruit!). The choice of rye crust is because rye crusts are my hearty, nutty favorites. You do sacrifice some gluten development, so I roll out rye crusts a bit thicker than normal pastry crust to give the fruit and caramel a sturdy base.

Rye Pastry Dough
(recipe follows)

APPLE FILLING

2 large apples (1½ pounds total), such as Gala or Honeycrisp, but any will do

1 tablespoon / 12g dark brown sugar

Diamond Crystal kosher salt

1 tablespoon / 14g salted butter

VINEGAR CARAMEL

¼ cup / 60ml apple cider vinegar

¼ cup / 50g dark brown sugar

1 tablespoon / 14g salted butter

Diamond Crystal kosher salt

2 tablespoons / 30ml heavy cream

Ice cream or whipped cream, for serving

1. Make and chill the dough as directed.

2. Make the apple filling: Cut the apples into paper-thin slices. Transfer to a large bowl and toss with the sugar and ¼ teaspoon salt.

3. Set a small saucepan over medium heat and add the butter. Let it begin to brown, 2 to 4 minutes. Pour directly over the apple slices and mix everything together. Set aside.

4. Position a rack in the center of the oven and preheat it to 375°F. Line a sheet pan with parchment paper.

5. Roll out the dough on a lightly floured surface into a round 14 inches in diameter. Transfer the crust to the lined sheet pan. Place the apple slices in the center, arranging them in any pattern that calls to you and leaving 2 inches open around the edges. Fold over the edges to encase the apples and move the galette to the fridge to chill until the oven is done preheating.

6. Begin the vinegar caramel: Wipe out the small saucepot and add the vinegar. Bring it to a boil over medium-high heat and let it simmer until the vinegar has reduced by half, 10 to 11 minutes.

7. Add the brown sugar, butter, and ¼ teaspoon salt and stir to combine. Turn down the heat to maintain a simmer and continue to cook, whisking often, until it has become syrupy and thickened slightly, 6 to 8 minutes. Whisk in the cream and set aside to cool. This yields ¼ cup of caramel, which will thicken more as it cools.

Recipe continues

8 . Before baking, brush *only* the exposed galette crust edges with the caramel, reserving the rest for later (if you brush the apples before baking, they become unbearably tart). Bake the galette until the crust is deeply golden and the fruit is bubbling on the edges, 40 to 45 minutes.

9 . Remove the pan from the oven and brush the caramel all over the top of the fruit. The residual heat will let it melt into the galette. Slice and serve with ice cream or whipped cream.

RYE PASTRY DOUGH

Makes enough for 1 standard-size piecrust or galette crust

7 tablespoons / 65g dark rye flour

1 cup plus 2 tablespoons / 160g all-purpose flour, plus more for dusting

Diamond Crystal kosher salt

12 tablespoons / 170g salted butter, chilled

5 tablespoons / 75ml ice water

1 . In a large bowl, whisk together both flours and 1 teaspoon salt. Add the butter in cubes and use your hands to toss and coat the butter in flour, then press each cube into disks, flattening and cutting into the flour until all the butter is well coated and no size is bigger than a bean. Working quickly, whisk in 4 tablespoons (60ml) of the ice water and use your hands to form a shaggy dough. Add the remaining 1 tablespoon (15ml) ice water if needed. Transfer the dough to a lightly floured work surface, pat it into a disk 1 inch thick, and sprinkle any butter pockets with more flour to seal them up. Cut the dough into thirds, layer them on top of one another, and press down to flatten the dough until it's 1 inch thick again. Rotate 90 degrees and repeat. This creates lamination and flaky, buttery layers.

2 . Wrap the disk in plastic wrap, then use a rolling pin to roll it out into the edges of the plastic wrap, making a smooth dough. Place it in the fridge to chill and hydrate. It needs at least 45 minutes, but the longer, the better.

GREEN TEA COFFEE CAKE

Makes one 8-inch square cake

My big vacation ritual is doing the whole pastry-case-for-breakfast thing. Although I'm never reaching for the croissant or the Danish, I'm usually headed for the giant cookie, the muffin, or, of course, the coffee cake. The fact that someone created a cake designed for breakfast eating is something that I need to formally thank them for—and I try to, with this cake! I took the cinnamon-y, wonderfully blank canvas of coffee cake and added a hint of matcha. It makes the cake feel extra breakfast-y, even though you have my permission to eat it any time of the day.

MATCHA CAKE

¾ cup / 150g granulated sugar

8 tablespoons / 113g salted butter, at room temperature

2 large eggs

½ cup / 120ml crème fraîche

1½ cups / 210g all-purpose flour

1½ teaspoons baking powder

2 teaspoons ceremonial-grade matcha

Diamond Crystal kosher salt

CINNAMON FILLING

2 heaping tablespoons / 35g granulated sugar

1 tablespoon / 12g dark brown sugar

1 tablespoon / 9g all-purpose flour

½ teaspoon ground cinnamon

MATCHA CRUMBLE

⅔ cup / 105g all-purpose flour

4 tablespoons / 60g granulated sugar

1 teaspoon ceremonial-grade matcha

6 tablespoons / 85g salted butter, chilled

1. Position a rack in the center of the oven and preheat it to 350°F. Line the bottom and sides of an 8 by 8-inch baking pan with parchment paper.

2. Make the cake: In a stand mixer fitted with the paddle attachment, beat together the sugar and butter at medium-high speed until light and fluffy, 3 to 4 minutes.

3. In a small bowl, whisk together the eggs and crème fraîche. Pour this into the butter mixture. Mix on medium speed to combine, scraping down the sides as needed.

4. In a large bowl, whisk together the flour, baking powder, matcha, and 1 teaspoon salt. Add this to the wet ingredients and mix on the lowest setting to combine.

5. Make the filling: In a small bowl, whisk together both sugars, the flour, and cinnamon.

6. Pour two-thirds (400g) of the batter into the lined baking pan. Spread the batter to the edges (it'll be thick!) and sprinkle the cinnamon filling evenly over the top. Dot the rest of the batter on top of the cinnamon filling, then spread it out so that it evenly covers the filling layer.

7. Make the crumble: In a medium bowl, whisk together the flour, granulated sugar, and matcha. Cube in the butter and use your fingers to toss the butter pieces to coat in the flour, then pinch and flatten them into pieces no bigger than a bean, creating a chunky, gravelly texture. Scatter the crumble evenly over the batter, reaching all the way to the edges. Bake until a toothpick inserted comes out clean, 40 to 45 minutes.

8. Let cool to room temperature before slicing; otherwise, you risk losing some of the crumble and that clean-cut look.

TINY SALTED TIRAMISU COOKIES

Makes 21 tiny cookies

These cute little cookies have all the flavor of tiramisu and none of the fuss. I use ground coffee to infuse them with concentrated flavor that I promise isn't grainy, but instant espresso powder also works. Then comes mascarpone's big moment: The Italian cream cheese gives the cookies a nice tang as well as a tender, soft chew and takes the place of an egg (similar to My Favorite Sour Cream Cookies on page 252, which you can make with any leftover mascarpone for bonus points). Serve these with a little glass of amaro and tell me I'm not wrong—they really do taste like tiramisu.

8 tablespoons / 113g salted butter, at room temperature

3 tablespoons / 40g packed dark brown sugar

½ cup / 110g granulated sugar

1 tablespoon rum

1 teaspoon ground coffee

3 tablespoons / 50g mascarpone cheese

1¼ cups / 175g all-purpose flour

Diamond Crystal kosher salt

1 teaspoon baking powder

4 ounces / 37g dark chocolate, finely chopped

Flaky salt, for topping

1 tablespoon Dutch processed cocoa powder, for topping

1. Equally stagger two racks in the oven and preheat it to 375°F. Line two baking sheets with parchment paper,

2. In a stand mixer fitted with the paddle attachment, cream together the butter, brown sugar, and granulated sugar until smooth, 2 to 3 minutes.

3. Add the rum, coffee, and mascarpone and beat on medium speed until the dough noticeably lightens in color and doubles in size, another 3 to 4 minutes. It will look whipped.

4. While the wet ingredients are mixing, in a small bowl, whisk together the flour, ½ teaspoon kosher salt, and the baking powder.

5. In two rounds, add the dry ingredients to the wet, with the mixer at its lowest speed to combine. Add the chocolate to the dough and fold this in by hand with a spatula.

6. Roll the dough into twenty-one tablespoon-size balls (25g each). Space the cookies 2 inches apart on lined baking sheets. Indent each in the center to encourage equal spreading. Sprinkle with the lightest touch of flaky salt.

7. Bake the cookies until the tops are crinkly and the cookies have spread, 9 to 10 minutes.

8. Remove the cookies from the oven and give the trays a few smacks on the counter to flatten the cookies out. While the cookies are still warm, use a cookie cutter or biscuit cutter to swirl around the cookies to make them into perfect circle (optional, for those who like perfection).

9. Let the cookies cool for 20 minutes. Use a sifter or small sieve to dust the cocoa powder over the top before serving.

BERRIES & CHERRIES UNDER CORN BREAD CAKES

Makes one 9 by 13-inch baking dish

Fluffy shortcake meets corn bread in this blend I'm calling corn bread cakes. And yes, we are dipping into cake *and* cobbler territory, but when their texture is this good, please don't blame me for semantics.

CORN BREAD CAKES

1 cup / 140g all-purpose flour

1 cup / 140g yellow cornmeal

2 teaspoons baking powder

1 tablespoon plus 2 teaspoons / 25g sugar

Diamond Crystal kosher salt

½ teaspoon grated lemon zest (about ¼ lemon)

8 tablespoons / 113g salted butter, chilled

1 cup / 240ml buttermilk

FRUIT TOPPING

2 pounds / 906g assorted berries such as blueberries, strawberries, raspberries

1 pound / 453g sour cherries, pitted and halved

½ teaspoon grated lemon zest (about ¼ lemon)

3 tablespoons / 45g sugar

1 tablespoon / 8g cornstarch

2 tablespoons fresh lemon juice (about ½ lemon)

BUTTERMILK WHIPPED CREAM

¼ cup / 60ml buttermilk, plus more for brushing

1 cup / 240ml heavy cream

1 teaspoon vanilla extract

1 tablespoon / 14g sugar

1. Make the corn bread cakes: Position a rack in the center of the oven and preheat it to 400°F.

2. In a large bowl, whisk together the flour, cornmeal, baking powder, sugar, 1½ teaspoons salt, and the lemon zest. Cube the butter and add it to the dry ingredients, tossing and flattening it with your fingers until it is cut into the dry ingredients and no butter piece is bigger than a bean.

3. Make a well in the center and add the buttermilk. Using a wooden spoon, mix into a sticky, soft dough. Put the bowl in the fridge while you prepare the fruit.

4. Prepare the fruit topping: Add the berries and cherries to a 9 by 13-inch baking dish and sprinkle with the lemon zest. Add the sugar, cornstarch, and lemon juice and stir to combine. Layer the fruit evenly so the baking dish is completely covered.

5. Use a damp hand to scoop up the corn bread cake dough into ⅓-cup portions, flatten them slightly before placing them all over the fruit. I usually end up with six to eight cakes. Evenly space them out and brush the tops with more buttermilk to encourage browning.

6. Bake until the cakes are golden and the fruit is bubbling, 40 to 45 minutes.

7. Meanwhile, make the buttermilk whipped cream: In a stand mixer fitted with the whisk attachment or with a hand mixer, combine the buttermilk, cream, vanilla, and sugar and beat on medium-high speed until stiff peaks form, 2 to 3 minutes. Store this in the fridge until the cakes are out of the oven.

8. Let the baking dish cool for a few minutes before serving everything together.

A VERY GOOD ORANGE TRUFFLE BROWNIE

Makes one 8 by 8-inch pan

Eric, my fiancé, introduced me to two big food revelations when we first met: (1) that it *is* humanly possible for someone to be a chocaholic and (2) that Pillsbury sells "Orange Rolls," which are cinnamon rolls with orange icing. Both are still revelations to me, but seven years later, here I am, making a recipe combining his two favorite flavors. This recipe is absolutely death-by-chocolate, balanced by some strong notes of orange woven throughout. After you let the brownies cool (see the tip on page 260), they slice into dense squares with a trufflelike bite. And even though I'm not a chocolate lover, this recipe gets a highly coveted place in this book, because I made it for my favorite person in the world.

¼ cup / 28g Dutch processed cocoa powder

6-ounces / 170g semisweet chocolate

10 tablespoons / 141g salted butter

¾ cup / 165g sugar

1 large egg

2 tablespoons / 30g crème fraîche

2 tablespoons fresh orange juice

⅔ cup plus 1 tablespoon / 100g all-purpose flour

Diamond Crystal kosher salt

1 tablespoon grated orange zest

1 . Position a rack in the center of the oven and preheat it to 350°F. Line the bottom and sides of an 8 by 8-inch baking pan with parchment paper.

2 . In a large heatproof bowl that fits over a large pot to make a double boiler, combine the cocoa powder, 1 bar (4 ounces / 113g) of the chocolate, the butter, and sugar. Set the pot over medium heat and add a few inches of water. Bring the water to an aggressive simmer, set the bowl over the top, and stir constantly to melt everything together. You'll want to be on top of it, since this will take some time, and you don't want the chocolate or sugar to burn.

3 . In a medium bowl to the side, whisk together the egg, crème fraîche, and orange juice.

4 . When the chocolate mixture has fully melted, stir for another 30 seconds or so before moving the pot to the counter. If you taste it at this point, the sugar should still taste grainy. Let this cool for a few minutes to go from hot to warm.

5 . Gradually drizzle the egg mixture into the chocolate mixture, whisking constantly. The batter should still be warm when you mix in the flour, 1 teaspoon salt, and the orange zest. Chop the remaining ½ bar (2 ounces / 57g) of chocolate and mix it into the warm batter; it's okay if it melts a bit.

6 . Pour the batter into the lined baking pan and bake until the top of the brownies is shiny and cracked and you can insert a toothpick and it comes out clean, 25 to 30 minutes.

7. Smack the pan on the counter a few times after baking to ease it into its wrinkly top. Let cool on the counter for 30 minutes or until the pan is cool to the touch, then transfer the pan to the fridge and let cool for another 45 minutes, or until the bottom of the pan is completely cold. This chilling is what gives the brownie its signature truffle-y chew.

8. Slice and serve.

BUTTERNUT SQUASH CAKE WITH CINNAMON WHIPPED CREAM

Makes one 9-inch loaf

My friend's husband has a family farm in upstate New York, and every fall they return with crates upon crates of winter squash. Going to their small apartment, it is almost comical to be offered four to seven squash to take home like a party favor. One winter, our abundance of gifted squash left me no choice but to make something that tasted like Christmas. This recipe is a take on my brown butter banana bread, one of my most popular recipes, but I substituted squash for the banana and added rye flour and a few extra spices to amp up the coziness. So, while I don't have a farm upstate with thousands of squash, this cake makes me feel as if I do.

8 tablespoons / 113g salted butter

¾ cup / 150g plus 1 tablespoon sugar

2 large eggs

1 teaspoon vanilla extract

2 cups / 330g cooked and mashed butternut squash (canned squash puree also works)

1½ cups / 220g dark rye flour

2½ teaspoons baking powder

1 teaspoon ground cinnamon

½ teaspoon ground allspice

Diamond Crystal kosher salt

1 cup / 240ml heavy cream, chilled

1 . Position a rack in the center of the oven and preheat it to 375°F. Line the bottom and sides of a 9 by 5-inch loaf pan with parchment paper.

2 . Set a small saucepan over medium heat and add the butter. Melt the butter, then let it foam and cook, stirring occasionally until flecks of brown form at the bottom of the pan, 4 to 6 minutes. Transfer the brown butter to a medium bowl and whisk to let it cool.

3 . Whisk ¾ cup of the sugar into the brown butter. Crack in the eggs and add the vanilla. Whisk vigorously into a smooth mixture. Add the squash directly into the bowl (there might still be chunks, but that's fine) and whisk to combine. Switch to a spatula and fold in the flour, baking powder, ½ teaspoon of the cinnamon, the allspice, and 1 teaspoon salt. Stir to combine into a nice, thick batter.

4 . Scrape the batter into the lined loaf pan and bake until a toothpick inserted comes out clean, 50 to 55 minutes. Let cool for 10 minutes before removing the cake from the pan onto a wire rack. Continue to let cool for at least another 30 minutes before serving.

5 . While the cake is baking, in a stand mixer fitted with the whisk attachment or with a hand mixer, combine the heavy cream, the remaining ½ teaspoon cinnamon, and the remaining 1 tablespoon sugar and beat on medium-high speed until stiff peaks form, 2 to 3 minutes. Chill the cream in the fridge until the cake is ready.

6 . To serve, slice the cake and serve with the cinnamon whipped cream.

ACKNOWLEDGMENTS

First, to everyone who has ever followed me on TikTok, Instagram, YouTube, Substack, Pinterest, my blog, or one of the many places I share my work. You—this one is for you. You made this possible. You are the reason I do what I do, you fill me purpose and joy, and I'm honored I get to spend time with you every day. I wrote this book for you all, and I hope it's everything you wanted. I hope we can make many more.

To Eric. This book was built by a lot of people, but it was you who consistently built me up while I wrote it. Thank you for tasting every brownie, hearing every headnote, and holding me together through it all. No word would exist if it wasn't for you. I don't know how I got so lucky to have you in my life and in these pages. I love you.

To my manager, Lisa Poe. You light a fire in me every day. You make me want to be better. You calm me and push me and keep me all together. You *found* me. I proudly call you my secret weapon, my lizard queen, and my cheerleader from day one. Thank god you're married, or else I would have proposed a long time ago. It's soul mate energy.

To my editor, Susan Roxborough. From our first meeting I knew you were the one I wanted to shepherd this book into the world. Thank you for your patience. Thank you for trusting me. Thank you for seeing my first bad "pancake" and still believing in where our book would go. And thank you for encouraging me to put my name on the cover. You found the spirit of this book and made it real.

To my agent, Sarah Smith. Wow, are you good at your job. Choosing to work with you was the easiest decision, and you made me feel supported from the start. Thank you for being the biggest advocate, sounding board, and protector. I'll sing your praises until the end of the world.

To Alex Beggs. You don't know it, but you saved the book. Thank you for being the first person to tell me to stop apologizing for my recipes and for being the one to inject me with confidence when I needed it the most.

To Casey Elsass. I knew my book had a soul, but you gave it a voice. Thank you for being a listening ear, the warmest presence, and the most helpful guide as I navigated through the book process. You're right, cookbooks are a foreign language, and you definitely speak fluently.

To my photographer, Jim Henkens. I was enamored with your work from the start. Thank you for taking a chance on this book and for making my recipes shine in a light that I could never imagine. Also, thank you for letting me use your porch. And your kitchen. And your dog.

To my food stylist, Frances Boswell. I can confirm you are the coolest person I know. Thank you for introducing me to Lost Bread's croissants, thank you for teaching me how to find the prettiest herbs, and thank you for breathing beautiful life into my recipes. They'll never look as good as when you cook them.

To my prop stylist, Brooke Deonarine. You saw my world and you jumped right in. Thank you for bringing the vibrance to set, both with your wonderful energy and with those yellow glasses that I will continue to obsess over until the day I die. Thank you for teaching me that it's okay to play around, and that blue might be my favorite color.

To food styling assistants Young Gun Lee and Sofia Toddeo. I repeat: I could not have done this without you. Your expert presence during our photoshoot shows up in the food. The positive energy is apparent on the page, and I'm forever grateful.

To my recipe testers, Julie Bishop and Jenn De la Vega. You kept me in check, kept me honest, and made sure that these recipes work to a T. It's no small task, and your diligence and detail were invaluable. I can confidently put these recipes out into the world because of you.

To every recipe tester from my audience and community. Thank you so much for your thoughtful input, your realistic tweaks (okay YES, dried limes aren't everywhere, we adjusted!), and your genuine enthusiasm and excitement for this book. I can't wait to get it in your hands!

To the designers of these pages, Marysarah Quinn and Mia Johnson. It's beautiful, and you know it is! Marysarah, thank you for your patience with my never ending questions and requests—you're a true craftsman (and wizard!) of these pages. And Mia, thank you for being the first to take what was just a Word document and transform it into a beautiful book. You've both turned me into a font nerd, in the best way.

To Ashley Pierce, Elaine Hennig, Jessica Heim, Alexandra Noya, Brianne Sperber, and Natalie Yera-Campbell at Clarkson Potter, as well as the team at Sprouthouse Agency. Thank you for building my book from beginning to end and for helping me usher it into the world. Francis Lam, thank you for taking me to coffee and leaving me with no doubt that Potter was the place I belonged. Jill Flaxman and Aaron Wehner, thank you for your wholehearted support and belief in my work.

To Bianca Cruz and Ezra Kupor. Bless you two for being the first to slide into my DMs and ask, "Have you thought about a book?" Turns out, I hadn't. But look at us now! Thank you for seeing what I didn't see.

To Liz Moody and Carina Wolff. Thank you for being my mentors but most of all, my friends. Our group chat carried me through this book process more than you know, and I'll always be grateful for it. But no, I'm still not moving to California.

To Joshua McFadden. You didn't expect to be in here, right? But I'll never forget the day I picked up *Six Seasons* in a thrift store, and it taught me how to cook. Thank you for showing me what an Italian salsa verde is. Thank you for starting Butter Boards. I'll always love a butter board.

To Joanne Schioppi, Kristin Brown, Debbie Sullivan, Aimee Buck, Stephanie Sarcona, and Caryn Schlossberg. Thank you for kicking me out of the nest with grace; for being there when it all started.

To Alayna and Luke. Can we all just agree to stay in one place for a bit? Just kidding. I love you both. Thank you for listening to my rants and replying to my frantic texts. Thank you for being proud of me. Thank you for being a part of me. We'll cook the roux until it's black next Christmas.

And to my Dad. I hope it's what you imagined. I hope everything is okay. And mostly, I hope the stovetops are really nice up there.

WORDS ON MY KITCHEN FRIDGE, WORDS I COOK BY

COOK IT SCARED

COOK HAPPY

COOK FOR ONE

OR MILLIONS

BUY THE OCTOPUS

USE YOUR CAMERA

FAIL BIG

EAT BIGGER

IF IT'S NOT RIGHT

IT'S PROBABLY ACID OR FAT

PLAY RESTAURANT

PLATE MESSY

BE GENTLE WITH YOUR TIME

PAUSE

TASTE

ROUND IT OUT

GET PERSONAL

HOME IS WHERE THE FIRE IS

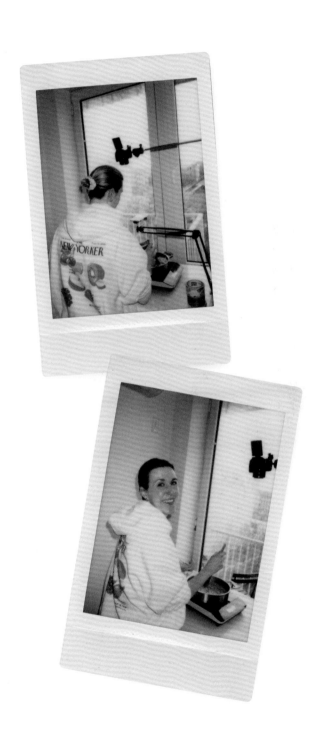

INDEX